THE MAGIC MONASTERY

D1022630

by the same author

SEEKER AFTER TRUTH
DESTINATION MECCA
THE SUFIS
SPECIAL PROBLEMS IN THE STUDY OF SUFI IDEAS
THE EXPLOITS OF THE INCOMPARABLE MULLA NASRUDIN
TALES OF THE DERVISHES
CARAVAN OF DREAMS
THE PLEASANTRIES OF THE INCREDIBLE MULLA NASRUDIN
REFLECTIONS
THINKERS OF THE EAST
A PERFUMED SCORPION
LEARNING HOW TO LEARN
THE HUNDRED TALES OF WISDOM
NEGLECTED ASPECTS OF SUFI STUDY
SPECIAL ILLUMINATION: THE SUFI USE OF HUMOUR
A VEILED GAZELLE: SEEING HOW TO SEE
THE ELEPHANT IN THE DARK
WISDOM OF THE IDIOTS
THE DERMIS PROBE
THE BOOK OF THE BOOK
THE WAY OF THE SUFI
THE SUBTLETIES OF THE INIMITABLE MULLA NASRUDDIN
WORLD TALES
KARA KUSH
DARKEST ENGLAND
THE NATIVES ARE RESTLESS

THE
MAGIC
MONASTERY

Analogical and Action Philosophy of the Middle East
and Central Asia

IDRIES SHAH

THE OCTAGON PRESS
LONDON

Copyright © 1972, 1981 by Idries Shah

All rights reserved
Copyright throughout the world

No part of this publication may be reproduced or transmitted in any form or by any means, electronic, mechanical or photographic, by recording or any information storage or retrieval system or method now known or to be invented or adapted, without prior permission obtained in writing from the publishers, The Octagon Press Ltd., except by a reviewer quoting brief passages in a review written for inclusion in a journal, magazine, newspaper or broadcast.

Requests for permission to reprint, reproduce, etc., to:
Permissions Department, The Octagon Press Ltd.,
P.O. Box 227, London N6 4EW, England

Reprinted with the aid of a subvention
from The Sufi Trust

ISBN 0 863040 58 6

First Published 1972
First impression in this Edition 1991

Printed and bound in Great Britain by
Redwood Press Limited, Melksham, Wiltshire

Contents

Preface

IN previous collections, like *The Dermis Probe* and *Thinkers of the East*, I have assembled tales illustrating the instructional methods employed by the Middle Eastern sages during the last thousand years, culled from both oral and written sources. *The Magic Monastery*, however, differs from its predecessors in one important respect.

This presentation of largely unpublished work contains not only traditional tales, but also pieces in the traditional format which I have composed myself when I have been unable to find an extant example to introduce at the point where Sufic comprehensiveness demands one. The book therefore consists of a representative cross-section of Sufi teaching which constitutes a harmonized whole, rather than a selection of typical extracts.

The number of orientalists and other scholars who have accorded generous recognition of earlier collections on technical and academic grounds requires grateful acknowledgment. No less important is the encouragement which people in the literary world have given, largely by directing attention to the intrinsic power of the materials in this tradition.

In addition, however, to the historical and aesthetic elements, I have myself always been concerned with the functional aspects of the action literature of the Sufis. It is, therefore, particularly gratifying to be able to record that this part of the work has recently been receiving increased attention and understanding. *The Magic Monastery* aims at contributing as much towards this last objective as towards the enjoyment of the general reader.

IDRIES SHAH

The Magic Monastery

A CERTAIN quiet dervish used often to attend the weekly meals given by a cultivated and generous man. This circle was known as 'The Assembly of the Cultured'.

The dervish never took part in the conversation, but simply arrived, smilingly shook hands with all present, seated himself in a corner, and ate the food provided.

When the meeting was over, he would stand up, say a word of farewell and thanks, and go his way. Nobody knew anything about him, though when he first appeared there were rumours that he was a saint.

For a long time the other guests thought that he must indeed be a man of sanctity and knowledge, and they looked forward to the time when he might impart some of his wisdom to them. Some of them even boasted of his attendance at their meetings to their friends, hinting at the special distinction which they felt at his presence.

Gradually, however, because they could feel no relationship with this man developing, the guests began to suspect that he was an imitator, perhaps a fraud. Several of them felt uncomfortable in his presence. He seemed to do nothing to harmonize himself with the atmosphere, and did not even contribute a proverb to the enlightened conversation which they had come to prize as a necessary part of their very lives. A few, on the other hand, became unaware that he was there at all, since he drew no attention to himself.

One day the dervish spoke. He said:

'I invite all of you to visit my monastery, tomorrow night. You shall eat with me.'

This unexpected invitation caused a change in the opinions

of the whole assembly. Some thought that the dervish, who was very poorly dressed, must be mad, and surely could provide them with nothing. Others considered his past behaviour to have been a test. At last, they said to themselves, he would reward them for their patience in bearing with such dreary company. Still others said to one another:

'Beware, for he may well be trying to lure us into his power.'

Curiosity led them all, including their host, to accept the hospitality.

The following evening the dervish led them from the house to a hidden monastery of such size and magnificence that they were dazed.

The building was full of disciples carrying out every kind of exercise and task. The guests passed through contemplation-halls filled with distinguished-looking sages who rose in respect and bowed at the dervish's approach.

The feast which they were given surpassed all powers of description.

The visitors were overwhelmed. All begged him to enrol them as disciples forthwith.

But the dervish would only say, to all their entreaties:

'Wait until the morning.'

Morning came and the guests, instead of waking in the luxurious silken beds to which they had been conducted the night before, clad in gorgeous robes, found themselves lying stiff and stark, dispersed on the ground within the stony confines of a huge and ugly ruin, on a barren mountainside. There was no sign of the dervish, of the beautiful arabesques, the libraries, the fountains, the carpets.

'The infamous wretch has tricked us with the deceits of sorcery!' shouted the guests. They alternately condoled with and congratulated one another for their sufferings and for having at last seen through the villain, whose enchantments obviously wore off before he could achieve his evil purpose, whatever that might be. Many of them attributed their escape to their own purity of mind.

But what they did not know was that, by the same means which he had used to conjure up the experience of the monastery, the dervish had made them believe that they were abandoned in a ruin. They were, in fact, in neither place.

He now approached the company, as if from nowhere, and said:

'We shall return to the monastery.'

He waved his hands, and all found themselves back in the palatial halls.

Now they repented, for they immediately convinced themselves that the ruins had been the test, and that this monastery was the true reality. Some muttered:

'It is as well that he did not hear our criticisms. Even if he only teaches us this strange art, it will have been worth while.'

But the dervish waved his hands again, and they found themselves at the table of the communal meal: which they had, in fact, never left.

The dervish was sitting in his customary corner, eating his spiced rise as usual, saying nothing at all.

And then, watching him uneasily, all heard his voice speak as if within their own breasts, though his lips did not move. He said:

'While your greed makes it impossible for you to tell self-deceit from reality, there is nothing real which a dervish can show you – only deceit. Those whose food is self-deceit and imagination can be fed only with deception and imagination.'

Everyone present on that occasion continued to frequent the table of the generous man. But the dervish never spoke to them again.

And after some time the members of the Assembly of the Cultured realized that his corner was now always empty.

Cat Think

ONCE upon a time there was a kitten.

Someone took him to see a tiger, fifty times his own size. The kitten said:

'Anyone who appears so large can have little real value. If he had anything in him, he wouldn't have to be so big.'

The Self-Congratulating Fruit

IT is related in the family of the Jan Fishanis that a certain Emir, attended by a substantial retinue, journeyed from Arabia to see the great Khan. When he arrived, he was treated with honour and given costly presents. Many of the court of Jan Fishan expected that after such a journey the prince would ask innumerable questions, or else remain mute and try to absorb wisdom through companionship with the great Khan.

But the Khan said, just before the Emir was ceremonially announced, 'Watch this interchange, for it is only rarely that one experiences such a thing.'

The Emir entered and said:

'Confirm me in my Emirate, for I am not of the Family of the Hashimites, and it is from your ancestors that all nobility receives its rank.'

Jan Fishan said:

'Do you wish ceremony and courtesy and the verification of rank, or do you seek an answer to a question?'

'Would that I could have both, but if only one is to be given, I desire an answer to my question,' said the Emir.

'Since you have asked, with absence of greed, for only one, I shall give you both,' said Jan Fishan Khan, 'and I shall confirm or deny your title in the answer to your philosophical question.'

The Emir asked:

'This is my question. Why do so many Sufis make light of the great deeds, the heroism, the patience and high-mindedness which is the heritage and the glory of the Arab?'

Jan Fishan said:

'And here is the answer, which will not only explain our

position but will also show you your own true position as a nobleman among the Arabs.

'We discount, and we even deride at times, the qualities upon which so many men pride themselves because those very qualities should be the minimum, not the maximum, attainable by man. If a man is a hero, or a patient one, or devout, or hospitable, or has any of the other qualities – this is the point from which he starts. Is he a beast, that he should be proud if he learns to conduct himself well in relation to others? Is he a fruit, that people should remember his name and always seek others of the same type? No, he is someone who should be ashamed that he has not always been worthy, and should be grateful that he is capable of great things.'

After this the nobleman abandoned the title of Emir, saying, 'Emir is the word we use for the kind of man who is at the bottom, so why should I need it to describe me? What we call an ordinary man, with few qualities, is not even to be counted in the Journey until he rises to what we call "Highness" (elevated).'

One of his companions said:

'What! Will you cast aside the glory of your family for something which you could have read in a book?'

The Emir said:

'I could have read it in a book, and it would have been no less true. Perhaps I have, indeed, read it in a book at some time, but I did not heed it. And, if I have in fact at some time read it, then I am doubly blameworthy, for I have betrayed my literacy through ignoring its value to me in helping me to change back to the status of man, from the status of a self-congratulating fruit.'

Greed, Obligement and Impossibility

A Sufi said:

'None can understand man until he realizes the connection between greed, obligement and impossibility.'

'This,' said his disciple, 'is a conundrum which I cannot understand.'

The Sufi said:

'Never look for understanding through conundrums when you can attain it through experience.'

He took the disciple to a shop in the nearby market, where robes were sold.

'Show me your very best robe,' said the Sufi to the shop-keeper, 'for I am in a mood to spend excessively.'

A most beautiful garment was produced, and an extremely high price was asked for it.

'It is very much the kind of thing I would like,' said the Sufi, 'but I would like some sequins around the collar, and a touch of fur trimming.'

'Nothing easier,' said the seller of robes, 'for I have just such a garment in the workroom of my shop.'

He disappeared for a few moments, and then returned, having added the fur and sequins to the self-same garment.

'And how much is this one?' asked the Sufi.

'Twenty times the price of the first one,' said the shopkeeper.

'Excellent,' said the Sufi, 'I shall take both of them.'

Delusion

A WOULD-BE disciple said to a sage:

'I have been listening to you for days now, condemning attitudes and ideas, and even conduct, which are not mine and never have been. What is the purpose of this?'

The sage said:

'The purpose of it is that you should, at some point, stop imagining that you have not been like any of the things I condemn; and to realize that you have a delusion that you are not like that now.'

Cat and Rabbit

A CAT said:

'Rabbits are not worth teaching! Here am I, offering cheap lessons in catching mice – and not a single rabbit taker!'

An Answer of Humanyun Adil

HUMANYUN ADIL heard someone say:

'If only this lecture by such-and-such a teacher contained more, were denser, how much more useful it would be!'

He immediately called out:

'That reminds me of the man who found a manuscript of four pages. He wished that there was no white space, thinking it a waste of paper.

'Suddenly the black of the letters increased, by magical effect. And soon every sheet of paper was completely black.'

The Disease

A NIGHTINGALE once said to a peacock:

'When I trill, people gather to listen to the beauty and purity of my voice – man may be a murderer but he is also an aesthete.'

The peacock listened well, and decided to get an admiring crowd for his beautiful plumage, something far more exquisite than anything that the nightingale could show.

So he went to a place where human beings congregated, and pranced in front of a group of people, folding and unfolding his tail, strutting and thrusting his feathers in front of everyone's eyes.

One of the men said:

'There is something wrong with that unfortunate peacock – he cannot keep still. It must be some illness.'

So they seized the peacock and killed it, in case the disease spread to their domestic fowls.

The Son of a Beggar

WHEN the Master Salim of Isfahan visited the town of Haidarabad in India, people vied with one another to be chosen as disciples.

Some were rich, others had a faultless knowledge of the Traditions, and everyone wanted to sit at the feet of Salim.

But when his visit was over, Salim left nobody to guide the people, and he took with him only the son of a beggar.

More than ten years later his deputy, Muzaffar, arrived in Haidarabad and resumed the Teaching there. Only when people realized his great worth did he reveal that he was the son of the beggar, chosen by Salim.

When this story became current, people told it as a marvel and regarded it as a lesson, but they saw only one side of it.

One day when he was at his open Court, someone said to Muzaffar:

'How poetic and just that the humblest should become the leader of all! Was it not painful to live in the atmosphere of the Master as the son of a beggar, and to endure the trials which come before one is transformed into a Sufi sheikh?'

Muzaffar said:

'For me it was somewhat painful. For one of my companions, whom I met there, however, it was really painful, for he was experiencing a greater change.'

They asked:

'And what were *his* origins? He must have been some sort of heretic.'

Muzaffar said:

'*He* was the son of a king.'

24

Three Epochs

1 *Conversation in the Fifth Century:*

'It is said that silk is spun by insects, and does not grow on trees.'

'And diamonds are hatched from eggs, I suppose? Pay no attention to such an obvious lie.'

'But there are surely many wonders in remote lands?'

'It is this very craving for the abnormal in the gullible which produces fantastic invention.'

'Yes, I suppose it is obvious when you think about it – that such things are all very well for the East, but could never take root in our logical and civilized society.'

2 *In the Sixth Century:*

'A man has come from the East, bringing some small live grubs.'

'Undoubtedly a charlatan of some kind. I suppose he says that they can cure toothache?'

'No, rather more amusing. He says that they can "spin silk". He has "brought them, with terrible sufferings, from one Court to another, having obtained them at the risk of his very life".'

'This fellow has merely decided to exploit a superstition which was old in my great-grandfather's time.'

'What shall we do with him, my Lord?'

'Throw his infernal grubs into the fire, and beat him for his pains until he recants. These fellows are wondrously bold. They need showing that we're not all ignorant peasants here, willing to listen to any wanderer from the East.'

3 *In the Twentieth Century:*

'You say that there is something in the East which we have not yet discovered here in the West? Everyone has been saying that for thousands of years. But in this century we'll try anything: our minds are not closed. Now give me a demonstration. You have fifteen minutes before my next appointment. If you prefer to write it down, here's a half-sheet of paper.'

A Sufi of Pamiristan

A SUFI from Pamiristan, Khwaja Tufa, was asked why he allowed people to praise him. He said:

'Some praise, some attack. We have no responsibility for those who praise – any more than we have for those who attack. They are quite independent of us, and do not in any case really heed us. Opposing the heedless is an empty activity. Those who neither praise nor attack us – some of those are people working with us and feeling with us. You do not see them, so you begin to concern yourself with praisers and opposers. This is a sort of bazaar where people are as it were buying and selling. The real activity is invisible to you.

'Looking at praise and attack is looking at irrelevancies. Irrelevancies are often more striking than relevancies. Interesting yourselves in the striking rather than the significant thing is usual but not useful.

'And do not neglect the address once given by Zilzilavi when he says:

' "I encourage fools to praise me. When they become extreme in this, they have at last an opportunity to observe the foolishness of fulsomeness. At the same time, those who are sickened by flattery will shun me, thinking that I encourage praise from desire of praise. But if they so lack perception that they can judge only by the surface, I must avoid them, for I am useless to them.

"The best of all ways of avoiding is to cause that which is to be avoided itself to avoid one, of its own desire." '

Last Day

A CERTAIN man believed that the last day for humanity would fall on a certain date, and that it should be met in an appropriate manner.

He gathered around him all who would listen. When the day came, he led them to the top of a mountain. As soon as they had assembled on the summit, their combined weight caused a collapse of its fragile crust, and they were all hurled into the depths of a volcano. It was indeed their last day.

Vine Thought

ONCE there was a vine which realized that people came every year and took its grapes.

It observed that nobody ever showed any gratitude.

One day a wise man came along and sat down nearby.

'This', thought the vine, 'is my opportunity to have the mystery solved.'

It said:

'Wise man, as you may have observed, I am a vine. Whenever my fruit is ripe, people come and take the grapes away. None shows any sign of gratitude. Can you explain this conduct to me?'

The wise man thought for a time. Then he said:

'The reason, in all probability, is that all those people are under the impression that you cannot help producing grapes.'

Appearances

A SUFI said:

'Such-and-such a Sufi reads all the books that he can find.'

A foreign visitor said:

'Why should he do that, since surely he must have the necessary knowledge already?'

'Because he wishes to couch his teaching in a language such as is being used at this moment. And because he constantly finds in modern books contemporary and arresting analogies with traditional materials.'

'But *you* do not employ modern analogies, so I assume that you do not read contemporary books,' said the visitor.

'But I do in fact read them, all that I can find.'

'Then why do you do so?'

'In order to *avoid* using current terminology. If I were to use it, people would instantly imagine that I have copied my thoughts from modern books.'

'But they do not do so in the case of the man you first mentioned.'

'That is because, although inwardly the same, his outwardness and mine are different. Many people judge only by external appearance. Until they trouble themselves to exercise another capacity, they will be at the mercy of appearance. Total disregard for this fact means that people are placed out of communication with us in reality and have to depend upon what they can obtain from our outwardness.'

Disguise

ONCE upon a time there was a bee who discovered that wasps did not know how to make honey. He thought he would go and tell them, but a wise bee said to him:

'Wasps do not like bees, and they would not listen to you if you approached them directly, since they are convinced – through age-old conviction – that bees are opposed to wasps.'

The bee thought about the problem for a long time, and then realized that if he covered himself with yellow pollen he would look so much like a wasp that they would accept him as one of them.

Now, representing himself as a wasp who had made a great discovery, the bee started to teach the wasps honey-making. The wasps were delighted, and worked well and hard under his direction.

Then there was pause for rest, and the wasps noticed that in the heat of the activity, the disguise had completely worn off the bee, and they recognized him.

With one accord, they fell on him and stung him to death as an interloper and ancient enemy: and, of course, all the half-made honey was abandoned ... for was it not the work of an alien?

Eating and Wonderment

THERE was once a Sufi who lived alone. He was sought out by a young man who wanted enlightenment, and he allowed him to come to live nearby, and said and did nothing to discourage him.

At length, having no teachings and little to think about, the young man said:

'I have never seen you eating, and I marvel at how you can sustain life without food.'

'Since you joined me,' said the Sufi, 'I have stopped eating in front of you. Now I eat in secret.'

The young man, even more intrigued, said:

'But why should you do that? If you wanted to deceive me, why should you now confess?'

'I stopped eating', said the sage, 'so that you might marvel at me, in the hope that you would one day stop marvelling at irrelevancies and become a real student.'

The young man asked:

'But could you not have simply told me not to marvel at superficialities?'

'Everyone in the world,' said the Sufi, 'and that includes you, has already been told precisely that, a hundred times at least. Do you imagine that one more handful of words on this subject would have had an effect on you?'

Pitcher Lore

HAVE you heard about the tragedy of the little pitcher?

He heard a thirsty man calling for water from his sick-bed in a corner of a room.

The pitcher was so full of compassion for the man that by a supreme effort of will he actually managed to roll to within an inch of the sufferer's hand.

When the man opened his eyes and saw a pitcher beside him, he was full of wonderment and relief. He managed to pick up the jug and held it to his lips. Then he realized that it was empty.

With almost the last remains of his strength, the invalid threw the pitcher against a wall, where it smashed into useless pieces of clay.

Exercises

It is related that Bahaudin Naqshband spoke in this way about exercises:

There are three phases of all exercises.

In the first, exercises are forbidden – the aspirant is not ready; exercises would harm him. This is the time when he generally desires exercises most.

In the second, when time, place and brethren are suitable for the exercises to have effect – exercises are indicated.

In the third, when exercises have had their effect – they are no longer needed.

And no Master ever performs exercises for his own progress on the way, for all Masters have passed the third stage.

Nectar

THE absence of sadness may create bitterness.

This saying is illustrated in the tale of the bee.

After a long winter, she found a flower-bed.

Three days later, the bee exclaimed:

'I cannot think what has happened to this nectar, it has become so sour.'

Absurdities

A CERTAIN Sufi sent all would-be disciples to hear and write down the harangues of his detractors, who for the most part were narrow-minded scholars.

Someone said:

'Why do you do this?'

He said:

'One of the first exercises of the Sufi is to see whether he can perceive the absurdities, partiality and distortions of those who imagine themselves to be men of wisdom. If they can really see through them in this way, descrying their selfish and bitter natures, then the disciples can begin to learn about Reality.'

Onions

A MAN without a sense of smell went to sleep on a bed of onions, wearing a magnificent robe.

When he got up, people fled from him in all directions.

'How lonely is the lot of the aesthete!' he lamented. 'Lacking sensitivity of sight, these people are depriving themselves of something superb.'

Tokens

VISITORS to the presence of Jan Fishan Khan were sometimes first welcomed by a man who spoke kind words to them. Then they were regaled with halwa. Just before being admitted to see the Khan, a piece of finest yellow gold was presented to them.

When they were presented to the Teacher, he said:

'Note the tokens which you have received. In our language they mean "If you want to harm a person, give him flattery, food and money." You can destroy him in this way, while he is fully occupied in thanking you for doing it.'

The Ass

'I KNOW that there will be clover when the weather improves,' said the ass, 'but I want it now. Everyone gets hay. How to solve the problem? I don't know, I'm too busy thinking about the clover.'

The Method

A CERTAIN seeker-after-truth approached one of the disciples of Mohsin Ardabili and said:

'Your master seems to pass his days in taking away from people their ideas and beliefs. How can anything good come of such behaviour?'

The disciple said:

'The jewel is found after the dirt has been removed from around it. The false jewel is made by applying layer after layer of impure substance, which nonetheless glitters, to any surface at all.

'The young vine is choked by weeds, yet nobody says, "Kill the vine, let the weeds flourish". The wrongdoer tries to throw the mantle of deception over his crime; but no one says, "Let the mantle be admired".'

The seeker-after-truth said:

'How can I have been so opaque that these considerations did not penetrate my mind? But why do you not publish these things more widely, so that all may benefit from this high knowledge?'

'It is published every day, in the behaviour of the Wise. It is contained in the books of the saints. It is manifested in tending gardens and making baubles. Do the heedless take notice of anything other than that which will increase their heedlessness?'

Nuts

A CAT said to a squirrel:

'How wonderful it is that you can so unerringly locate buried nuts, to nurture you through the winter!'

The squirrel said:

'What, to a squirrel, would be remarkable would be a squirrel who was *unable* to do such things.'

Visitors

IT is related that a man entered the presence of Gilani and said to him:

'O Great Sheikh! Why do you not see so-and-so, who has read all that you have written, who has discussed your sayings with your companions, and who wishes more than anything else to ask such-and-such a question?'

Gilani said:

'If I were to see him it would be a discourtesy on my part. His question is already answered in my writings, but he has not digested them.'

'But how is this a discourtesy? Surely it is an even greater courtesy to see such a necessitous one, so that you might put him on the right path, if he does not understand your writings.'

'Look out of that window,' said Gilani, 'where those three hundred or so people are waiting. All of them have read the written tracts; many of them come from far distances; many have sent in questions and await reception. Would there be no discourtesy to *them*?

'How would *you* feel if you were a worker who had performed a task and, instead of being paid, was kept waiting while a heedless man was given a payment instead of you? While your family waited at home for the breadwinner to return and give them love and the food which he had bought from his own sweat as a day-labourer, denying them his company and protection in order to earn it?'

Thirsty

THERE once was a king who was thirsty. He did not quite know what the difficulty was, but he said:

'My throat is dry.'

Lackeys at once ran swiftly to find something suitable to alleviate the condition. They came back with lubricating oil. When the king drank it, his throat did not feel dry any more, but he knew that something was not right.

The oil produced a curious sensation in his mouth. He croaked:

'My tongue feels awful, there is a curious taste, it is slippery ...'

His doctor immediately prescribed pickles and vinegar – which the king ate.

Soon he had stomach-ache and watering eyes to add to his sorrows.

'I think I must be thirsty,' he mumbled, for his sufferings had made him do some thinking.

'Thirst never made the eyes water,' said the courtiers to one another. But kings are often capricious, and they ran to fetch rosewater, and scented, syrupy wines fit for a king.

The king drank it all, but still he felt no better – and his digestion was ruined.

A wise man who happened along in the middle of this crisis said:

'His Majesty needs ordinary water.'

'A king could never drink common water,' shouted the court in unison.

'Of course not,' said the king, 'and, in fact, I feel quite insulted – both as a king being offered plain water and also as a patient. After all, it must be impossible that such a dreadful and daily more complicated ailment as mine could have a simple remedy. Such a concept is contrary to logic, a disgrace to its originator, and an affront to the sick.' That is how the wise man came to be renamed 'The Idiot'.

The Realm

ONE of the Sufi masters said to his companion:

'I have need of money to save the King, who must pay his troops.'

'But', said the companion, 'why does the King not get the money himself?'

'People must not know that the populace does not pay the taxes, otherwise a worse monarch might overcome the King.'

They set off on a journey to seek the money. At the first house at which they called, the householder said:

'Take everything I have, for I know you to be wise and good.' But the sage refused to take the money. His companion asked him why, and the master answered:

'Should I, to save a king, spoil a subject – who would after paying do anything he liked, believing that he has *bought* forgiveness?'

'Then why did we call at that house?'

'To see whether this man's inner life had progressed, whether he was yet a person who can give without buying …'

At the second house the master took one-half of the money which was offered to him. Again his companion asked him why he did not take it all, or refuse the money altogether.

'Because he will be impressed that we did not take all the money, and will listen to the next dervish who comes this way, who happens to be a true one.'

'And if we had refused *all* the money he would have been even more impressed?'

'Not this particular man, for he would have wondered why we were not attending to our mission, to find funds for the King.'

'What would you have done if you had known that the next dervish to call here were to be a false one?'

'I would have turned this man against us, to shield him against trusting dervishes for a time.'

After several weeks of this journey, they had collected the necessary amount of money. Now the companion said:

'I have been wondering why it is that you, a holy dervish, did not use occult powers to obtain money which was so urgently needed.'

The master said:

'One of the reasons was that *you* needed the lessons of this journey.'

'But', said the companion, 'if I am still asking you shallow questions, how can I have benefitted by the experiences?'

'This was the question which it was necessary for you to ask,' said the dervish, 'so that you might have the answer: "On this imperfect Earth, once you set foot here, you are bound to use imperfect methods, the methods of the Earth." To use special powers one has to be engaged in something of greater significance than obtaining the pay of an army: even though, as in this case, it is for the preservation of the stability of a realm.'

Vanity

A SUFI sage once asked his disciples to tell him what their vanities had been before they began to study with him.

The first said:

'I imagined that I was the most handsome man in the world.'

The second said:

'I believed that, since I was religious, I was one of the elect.'

The third said:

'I believed I could teach.'

And the fourth said:

'My vanity was greater than all these; for I believed that I could learn.'

The sage remarked:

'And the fourth disciple's vanity remains the greatest, for his vanity is to show that he once had the greatest vanity.'

Destitution

A MONKEY once said to a man:

'Do you not realize how destitute I am? I have no house, no clothes, no fine food like you, no savings, furniture, lands, articles of adornment – nothing at all. You, in contrast, have all these things and more. Besides, you are a rich man.'

The man felt ashamed. He made over everything he had to the monkey, beggaring himself.

When the monkey had taken legal charge of his entire possessions, the man said to him:

'Now what are you going to do with all this?'

The monkey said:

'Why should I talk to a penniless fool like you?'

Where it Starts

A CERTAIN Sufi master was walking along a country road with one of his disciples. The disciple said:

'I know that the best day of my life was when I decided to seek you out, and when I discovered that through your Presence I would find myself.'

The Sufi said:

'Decision, whether for support or opposition, is a thing which you do not know until you know it. You do not know it through thinking that you know it.'

The disciple said:

'Your meaning is obscure to me, and your statement is dark, and your intention is veiled from me.'

The master said:

'You will in a few moments see something about the value of decision, and who it is that makes decisions.'

Presently they came to a meadow, where a farm worker was throwing a stick to a dog. The Sufi said:

'I will count five, and he will throw three sticks to the dog.'

Sure enough, when the Sufi had so counted, the man picked up three sticks and threw them to the dog, even though they were out of earshot and the man had not seen the pair.

Now the Sufi said:

'I will count three, and the man will sit down.'

As soon as he had counted to three, the man did indeed sit down, suddenly, on the ground.

Now the disciples, full of wonder, said:

'Could he be induced to raise his arms into the air?'

The Sufi nodded and, as they watched, the man's hands rose towards the sky.

The disciple was amazed, but the Sufi said:

'Let us now approach this man and speak with him.'

When they had saluted the farm worker, the Sufi said to him:

'Why did you throw three sticks instead of one for the dog to retrieve?'

The farm man answered:

'I decided to do it as a test, to see whether he could follow more than one stick.'

'So it was your own decision?' 'Yes,' said the man, 'nobody told me to do it.'

'And', said the Sufi, 'why did you sit down so suddenly?'

'Because I thought I would rest.'

'Did anyone suggest it?'

'There is nobody here to suggest it.'

'And when you raised your arms in the air, why was that?'

'Because I decided that it was lazy to sit on the ground, and I felt that raising my arms towards the Heavens would indicate that I should work rather than rest, and that inspiration to overcome laziness came from on high.'

'Was that a decision of your own and nobody else's?'

'There was, indeed, nobody to make such a decision for me, and in any case it followed from my previous action.'

The Sufi now turned to the disciple and said:

'Immediately before this experience, you were saying to me that you were glad you had made certain decisions, such as the one that you should seek me out.'

The disciple was completely silent. But the farm worker said:

'I know you dervishes. You are trying to impress this hapless youth with your powers, but it is sure to be a form of trickery.'

Statistic

A POOR man said to a rich one:
   'All my money goes on food.'
   'Now that's your trouble,' said the rich man. 'I only spend five per cent of *my* money on food.'

Night and Morning

KHWAJA TILISM was a Sufi teacher who communicated his spirituality to dervishes at his centre entirely by 'thought-contact', which is sometimes called the heart-to-heart action.

In the studies, no word was spoken and no movement made.

One day a party of intending disciples arrived at the court, eager to take part in the ceremonies, the observances and the exercises which they expected would be the basis of the activities at this place, which was called the Taslim-Khana, the House of Resignation.

After they had been seen by one of the Khwaja's deputies and had had converse with him, they were shown into the Hall of Knowledge where elaborate ceremonial, complicated exercises and unusual music occupied their attention for many hours.

The following day all were called before the master. He asked them whether they felt uplifted by their experiences of the night before.

Seated in the centre of the hall, the visitors one by one declared that this had been one of the most sublime experiences of their lives. The resident dervishes stood against the walls, silently observing. Other guests were also present. When the visitors had completed their reports and concluded with pleas for acceptance as dervishes, the Khwaja spoke.

He first thanked his guests for their praise and for their wishes for his health and the continued prosperity of the House. Then he said:

'This morning there are three kinds of people among us. First are the "minute discerners", the dervishes who know what has happened and need no information about it. Second are the new arrivals, who may learn, from proximity, what has happened. Third are our guests of last night. It is you people whom I address in the tongue of man, for you will not hear the "speech of angels". You people have tasted of hospitality, ceremonial and boon-companionship. You have not tasted of spirituality here, whatever you may believe about this matter.

'We provided the entertainments and the hospitality so that those of you who wish for entertainment might not be disappointed; as should be the actions of good hosts. We also provided, as is the work of those who know, the Direct Communication. This was, and always remains, accessible. But it is and was accessible in this manner following:

'Not to those engaged in "tasting the world" in the name of pious observances. Their inner taste is useless. Not to those who might merely spurn the observances and imagine that the spurning itself makes them anything better. The derision destroys the inner capacity of taste. Only to those who really taste the wine without chewing the glass. It is those among you who really speak the language of the wine and not of the glass.

'We have had a period of noise in which the lips and tongue, the outward voice, have spoken to me of their outward experiences – the pleasure in exercises and ceremonials, and even of the pain of their searching.

'Now we shall have a space of silence, in which the inward voice of those in whom one is alive shall speak to our inwardness about the experiences which we have extended other than the music, food, repetitions and exercises.

'Those who ask with the inward voice shall be heard by the inward ear. Speak now, in that language.'

Man and Animal

THE mouse said:
  'I want to find crumbs.'
  The dog said:
  'I have come to find crusts.'
  The simpleton said:
  'What you need is bread, you fools!'
  The wise man said:
  'But you could let them have other kinds of food ...
  The simpleton was annoyed. He said:
  'The common denominator of their desires is bread, not food. You are becoming too complicated.'

Obvious

SIMAB, in his youth, said to a dervish whom he met sitting at the wayside:

'Would that I could do any solitary thing that would cause men to count me among the Saints.'

The dervish raised his head from his knee and instantly replied:

'That is the easiest thing in the world to do.'

Simab begged the dervish to tell him the secret.

The dervish said:

'Thousands of Sufis have been murdered by good people for saying things which those people did not like. All you have to do is to utter an incomprehensible remark. Then you will be doing at least one thing which couples your name with that of the greatest saint, Hallaj. Who would want more than that?

'If external behaviour and the beliefs of men made saints, there would be no earth, only a heaven full of obvious saints.'

Prisoner

A MAN was once sent to prison for life for something which he had not done.

When he had behaved in an exemplary way for some months, his jailers began to regard him as a model prisoner.

He was allowed to make his cell a little more comfortable; and his wife sent him a prayer-carpet which she had herself woven.

When several more months had passed, this man said to his guards:

'I am a metalworker, and you are badly paid. If you can get me a few tools and some pieces of tin, I will make small decorative objects, which you can take to the market and sell. We could split the proceeds, to the advantage of both parties.'

The guards agreed, and presently the smith was producing finely-wrought objects whose sale added to everyone's well-being.

Then, one day, when the jailers went to the cell, the man had gone. They concluded that he must have been a magician.

After many years when the error of the sentence had been discovered and the man was pardoned and out of hiding, the king of that country called him and asked him how he had escaped.

The tinsmith said:

'Real escape is possible only with the correct concurrence of factors. My wife found the locksmith who had made the lock on the door of my cell, and other locks throughout the prison. She embroidered the interior designs of the locks in the rug which she sent me, on the spot where the head is prostrated in prayer. She relied upon me to register this design and to realize that it was the wards of the locks. It was necessary for me to get materials with which to make the keys, and to be able to hammer and work metal in my cell. I had to enlist the greed and need of the guards, so that there would be no suspicion. That is the story of my escape.'

Characteristics

ONE of the great Sufis was asked:

'Whence comes this teaching, whose thoughts are you giving us, what is the name of your teacher?'

He answered:

'If I say it is from inspiration, I shall be a heretic. If I say it is my own, some will worship me and not heed it, others will criticize it and not heed me. If I name my teacher, all will turn to him and ignore real study.'

Someone said:

'Yet (and I seek pardon for saying this) you have named the great among the ancients as sources of the Teaching. Are we not in danger of turning to them and not to what they taught because of this?'

He replied:

'If, after being told a hundred times that all the teachers are one and that all names refer to characteristics, you still turn to personality, then you are in such danger.'

The man asked:

'Then what shall I do?'

The Sufi told him:

'Stop imagining that, because you can ask a question, you can perceive the answer without any of the qualities necessary for such perception to operate.'

Theoretician

ONCE upon a time there was a man of great repute for his wisdom, who lived in a certain town.

He told the people about life and death, about the planets and the earth, about history and about every kind of unknown thing.

One day a dam burst and the people went running to him to tell them how they could solve the problem.

The wise man drew himself up to his full height.

'I think that you should avoid asking such puerile questions from a man of the mind. I am not a water engineer, I am a theoretician.'

Catharsis

JAN FISHAN Khan heard that a certain narrow-minded scholar was bitterly attacking the culture, nature and ideas of one of his neighbours.

He invited both of them to a feast, and beforehand he said to the neighbour, 'Whatever I say tonight, make sure that you do not react to it in any way.'

After the meal, as is customary, the host started to orate.

He turned to the company and began to berate the very man whom the scholar was opposing. Without interruption for nearly an hour, he spoke of the man's supposed iniquities and enlarged, with quite unusual loquacity and totally devastating vituperation, upon the villainy and frightfulness of the victim.

Throughout this harangue nobody, including the neighbour, moved a muscle.

At the end of the outburst the scholar stood up and cried:

'In the Name of God, let us have no more of this! I saw my own behaviour in you just now, and I cannot bear the sight. This man's patience has destroyed me!'

Jan Fishan Khan said:

'In being here tonight we all took a chance. You that our friend here might attack you; I that you might have been further inflamed by my vituperation instead of being shamed by it; and he that he might start to believe that I really was against him. Now we have solved the problem. The risk remains that the account of this interchange, passed from mouth to ear by those who do not know what we were doing, will represent our friend as weak, you as easily influenced and me as easily angered.'

Fantasy

THE PROFESSOR said:

'Gentlemen. Among the most rewarding sides of psycho-anthropology is the analysis of myths and legends of primitive peoples. Such a study casts brilliant light upon the incapacities of undeveloped man, as well as upon his compensation-mechanism: how he invents marvels, magical substitutes for the fulfilments which he has never experienced.

'As an example, consider the ancient legend, met in many different communities, of the "camera". This instrument was supposed to be able to capture, in "frozen" form, events which were visible to the spectator, and to reproduce them, or a similitude of them, at will. I need hardly say that the entire conception of such an apparatus springs only from the very human desire to preserve moments of excitement and pleasure.

'Then there is the fable about the production of an energy of a special kind, in some languages called "electricity". This has truly wonderful wish-fulfilment properties. Why, by connecting to a supply of "electricity" different kinds of apparatus, man was reputed to have been able to cause heat or cold, to kill or to stimulate, to transmit the human voice for incalculable distances.

'There are, I regret to say, even today, sadly misled people who imagine that these legends contain what they like to call "a germ of truth". Some of them have even gone so far as to postulate reasons why they are likely to be true. But the explanations are always too bizarre. The wishful thinkers have to invent a myth or at the least graft one myth on to another. An instance is the answer of the cranks to the question: "Why are there no cameras or electrical contrivances now?" The answer is, of all amazing rationalizations, "Because at a certain time all the metal in the world was atomized, so we can't make them now." You observe that in order to sustain the fantasy, it has been necessary to invent a wondrous substance, known in the legends of some tribes as "metal".'

Kindness

A TEACHER gave a letter to his disciple, to be opened after his death and to be shown to his successor.

The letter said:

'I have been unkind to this disciple.'

When he heard the contents, the disciple was overcome with grief, and said:

'He was so generous that he saw his great kindness to me as cruelty, compared to the Greatest Kindness which might have been possible.'

A year or so later, the successor called the disciple to him again, and asked him to make a further comment on the letter.

'I now understand', said the disciple, 'that the word "unkind" was quite correct. Ordinary human beings show friendliness when they have nothing of greater value to impart. What need of kindness or cruelty from a Bestower of Treasures? If the Sultan's slave is handing over gold, what matters it if he smiles or frowns the while?

'The well-intentioned man may give away sweetmeats; the physician bestows curative medicine, whether people think the medicine is bitter or sweet.'

Misjudged

THERE was once a sage who had a considerable number of followers – and also many enemies.

The enemies resolved to kill him, and discovered that he allowed people to enter his house and wander all through it. They poisoned a number of apples, and left them in various rooms.

This happened several times: and after some months the poisoners were amazed to discover that the sage was still alive and well.

Some of them concluded that he was a saint of such subtle and complete perceptions that he had been able to avoid the apples, or even to eat poison without ill-effect.

They went to him and, throwing themselves on the ground, said:

'We realize that you must indeed be a saint, and wish to become your disciples.'

'Your grounds for supposing that I am a saint do not impress me,' said the sage, 'and if you are really interested, I have to tell you that I escaped your plot because I do not happen to eat fruit that I find lying about the house.'

Scratching

THERE was once a man who scratched himself.

His scratching became so extensive that people asked him why he did it. All he could say was 'I don't know.'

Physicians were called in, and none could find the source of the scratching.

After many years a wise man visited the town of the scratcher. The people brought the sufferer to the main square to show him to the sage.

There was a long pause. Then the wise man spoke:

'This individual', he said, 'is scratching. You have asked me to tell you the reason. I have applied my intellect to the problem, and I can give you the answer. The man scratches because he is itching.'

The Oatland Story

THERE was once a man who adopted oatmeal as the be-all and end-all of life. His reason for making this decision is not questioned by his numerous followers, because they came to hold this wisdom to be self-evident. Critics, who are sure to be biased, of course, have disputed whether it was because his name happened to be Avena, Latin for Oat, or whether he merely became obsessed by some form of self-flattery, based on his sense of the fitness of things.

He certainly liked oats, if we are to believe the ancient chronicles. To him they were beautiful, tasty, nutritious and versatile. He rapidly convinced many people of these and other advantages. He was, of course, marked by his idealism, logicality, dedication to the cause and exemplary life.

Even porridge, as he was easily able to demonstrate, gave scope for practical as well as theoretical applications, extension, inventions and even lyricism. He and his early associates cultivated oats, sniffed them powdered, applied them in various ways to the skin. Oats were soon found useful for such diverse things as glue, bricks, modelling, making paper, feeding rats and purposes of religious observance. Baked, sawed and coloured, treated in a thousand different ways, generations of tireless and heroic experimenters found the substance a means for the liberation of man and the enrichment of his life.

The diversity of oatish applications itself stimulated people to ever greater achievements. Who could doubt the value, and then inevitably the indispensability, of such a discovery? All civilization could be seen as built upon oats. The analogies, symbolism and other more refined relationships of oats, too, played a full part in human culture.

Even before many of these developments had taken place, the birth of Oatland was a foregone conclusion. Because of this unique flowering of the oatish genius, it was at first called 'The Land of Oats'. When, quite logically, the word 'oat' itself came to denote perfection, the country accepted the title of 'The Oat of Lands'.

Oatism became a valued and self-perpetuating system, because its results were proved by its assumptions and its assumptions were proved by its results.

A certain form of education was characteristic of Oatland. Naturally, it was the only form. Who would have built schools, if it had not been necessary to pass on oatishness? How could the civilization have developed without oats and without institutions which taught oatistically, so that the younger generation could benefit from the heritage of oatism for which so many had suffered and to build up which so many had laboured for so long?

If schools had not been devised, man would certainly have remained sunk in ignorance and depravity. It was inconceivable that any alternative would have developed. What alternative could there have been, since we all know that man needs oats, lives oats, thinks oats? Are oats not his dearest possession and guarantee of his sovereignty of thought? Does man's stomach not reject any other intrusion?

It has been suggested by would-be dissentients from oatism that man could, in fact, digest some other food than oats. The 'reasoning' behind this speculation is remarkably ingenious. It is held that man can digest only oats because he has eaten them for so long that this has become a 'limitation'. The dangerous nature of the corollary to this absurdity is that man could try to wean himself from oats, or else to eat, little by little, other things as well as oats. It is self-evident, however, that only the gullible and esotericist-unbalanced would be interested in such an attempt. The risk, too, is that the resultant certain starvation would cause early death.

(*Errors and Heresies*, Vol. 99, Oatland Defence Council publication, s.v. DIGESTION.)

Occasional trouble-makers and those who dared, it is true, said to the Oatlanders: 'Why not eat fruit?'

But they were soon told, with rapier-sharp logic: 'Fruit is repugnant to any freeborn Oatlander.'

Unthinking morons, too, were heard to say: 'Why not build with clay bricks?' When they got any reply at all (which was more than they deserved), it soon put them in their place.

'Clay is for moles. Besides, Avena the First, our glorious Founder, would have ordained and guided the use of clay if it had been of any use.'

When yet other adventurists said: 'Metal can be used to make tools,' they were told: 'A tool of porridge is a *real* tool. A porridge metal would be a *real* metal.'

But oatistic capacity was not limited to defending the porridge or tirelessly researching into its values and uses. The philosophy could challenge all comers with an unanswerable dialectic:

'If any of these crazy ideas outside oatism were capable of being useful in life, they could be explained in Oatlandese, the richest, most sublime medium of communication devised by man.'

On one occasion, an oatist theoretician said:

'You non-oatists are a mere rabble of mystics, esotericists, magicians, occultists, shamans, madmen, frustrated spinsters, gullible idiots, obsessionals and hopeless cases.'

'No, we are not,' said the non-oatists. But the thing to realize is that they mostly were, by an overwhelming majority.

And they were, ironically enough, because they had been driven that way by oatists.

Real non-oatists, as distinct from sensationalists, were compelled to organize themselves in a tight and discreet manner, for protection from the wilder oatists and the Oatland disaffected who clamoured for admission, claiming the name of unoatism and making more noise than anyone else.

The Oatlanders only had to point to this rabble – who couldn't even grow oats – virtually to prove that all non-oatists were deranged.

Meanwhile, of course, Oatism was producing a rich and promising culture. Some idea of its extent and inspirational value may be gleaned from even small quotations from its hoary wisdom.

When facts were short – or time limited – inspiration could come into its own, with such uplifting rallying-cries as:

'Ninety million Oatlanders can't be wrong.'

Nobody could accuse Oatlanders of being narrow-minded. Intense interest was aroused by genuinely new thoughts. One of the oatean philosophers demonstrated the continuing fecundity of the race by saying: 'I am a Porridgeman, therefore I exist!'

There was the occasional tyrant who said: 'Porridge? It is I!', but such people died sooner or later, leaving the beauty and validity of the thing unchallenged.

'Oatland for Ever' is one of the most touching of the traditional airs. Its opening words are:

'Graceful Oat, Holy Oat, Loving Oat, Giving Oat ... Oat! Oat! Oat!'

There were also revolutions in thought from time to time when the old sentimentalities were severely criticized. One such was when modernist writers explored the possibilities of new ways to express their inner being. The first few stanzas of a typical example of the New Poetry show how the vitality of the human spirit had been maintained:

> Oat,
> Ota,
> Aot,
> Tao.

The self-renewing sensation engendered by throwing off the

shackles of hidebound traditionalism in this manner must surely be unique.

Oatlandism, to be sure, employed arguments derived by sophistry and selection from its basic documents, to support its beliefs. If anyone else adduced other documents, they were quite fitly characterized as 'regressive' and 'unreliable'. Fresh interpretations of the Oatland Documents were accepted or otherwise according to whether the methods used were oatiferous or not.

Before dissentients were finally laughed into silence, some were reputed to have said: 'Don't abandon oats – but add other things to your life. You can do it.' The reaction was that they were malcontents or lying, trying to unsettle people.

Although society was continuously developing, some people always had an admiration for the old ways. Flowers used to be left on the statue of Avena the First and of the Oatist martyr who said: 'Take my body and soul – you will never get my oats!'

The conservative element, in this model open society where all forms of opinion were allowed free expression, said:

'If there were any alternative to oats, people would not have used them for 50,000 years, would they?'

The progressives, who disagreed, said:

'There is a simple, though different, alternative – it is porridge!'

The liberal element hoped for a compromise based on baked oatcakes as a way of life.

These are a few sayings preserved by this high culture as worthy of its greatest sons and daughters:

'If your oats are warm, use them as a plaster. If not, heat them!'

'Oats rhymes with goats. But otherwise the two are poles apart.'

'All that's sticky is not oats.'

'An oat a day keeps cornmeal away.'

*

What, if anything, eventually happened to the Oatlanders? I am afraid that I do not know.

Some people say that they died out. It seems more likely that such a calumny arose in the minds of their envious detractors ...

Zaky and the Dove

THERE was once a man named Zaky. Because of his capacities and his promise, a certain teacher – the Khaja – decided to help him. This Khaja assigned a subtle creature of special powers to attend upon Zaky and to help him whenever he could.

As the years passed, Zaky found that his material and other affairs prospered. He did not imagine that such advantages as he was receiving were entirely due to himself, and he started to notice a coincidence of events.

Whenever his affairs were about to go well, he observed, a small white dove was to be seen somewhere nearby.

The fact was that the subtle attendant, in spite of his powers, needed to be within a certain distance of Zaky to carry on his work. In spite of his remarkable abilities, in his transition into the present dimension he had to take a form. A dove was the form which he had adopted as most suitable.

But Zaky only connected doves with luck, and luck with doves.

So he started to keep doves, and to put down food for any dove which he saw, and to have doves embroidered on his clothes.

He became so interested in doves that everyone in the world thought him an authority on them. But his material and other affairs ceased to prosper, because his concentration had been diverted from intention to manifestation, and the subtle attendant in the form of a dove himself had to withdraw, to avoid becoming a cause of Zaky's undermining of himself.

Grass

A MAN once approached a group of farmers in a field, and said to them:

'Brothers, have you seen a good man pass this way? I am seeking my Master, who, not long ago, has come before me along the path.'

The farmers said:

'Yes, such a man, of impressive countenance yet simple manners, has indeed been here. Look, there is the mark of his foot, where the grass is flattened.'

The Seeker bent down reverently and picked a blade from the turf and held it admiringly in his hand.

The farmers laughed, and one said:

'See, he thinks he looks for the direction of his teacher, but really venerates a piece of grass.'

This man was so annoyed, so hurt was his vanity, that he imagined that by this well-meant and relevant rebuke the farmers intended discourtesy.

Instead of learning from the event, therefore, he said:

'Not one of us here is as honoured as this blade of grass, for it has touched the Master's feet.'

What had hurt him was the implication that he himself was a fool, not the suggestion that his Master was less important than he thought him to be; for no such intention nor statement was present in the farmers' words.

And the farmers, for their part, now felt themselves slighted by the charge that they were 'less than grass'. Their original benevolence towards the Seeker evaporated, and an argument started.

It is because of such tendencies that Seekers are called Seekers, and not Finders.

Prospects

RAMIDA agreed to talk to sixteen visiting dervishes in one afternoon.

One of his neighbours said:

'I regard you as a saint! You give your kindliness unstintingly and abundantly, even though you have other and pressing affairs to attend to.'

Ramida said:

'By insisting that they be seen at their own convenience, they have obtained satisfaction but no advantages. My affairs have been delayed by half a day. Their prospects have been postponed, perhaps, by years. Had I declined to see them, they would not have fared worse in the area of Reality.'

The Mirror, the Cup and the Goldsmith

A CERTAIN goldsmith worked for many years to perfect a magic mirror and a cup. The chief properties of these articles were that the mirror showed which of one's friends was in any trouble, and the cup enabled the user to dissolve troubles, by dropping a pebble into it. It could also make one rich.

The goldsmith, however, was unable to use the magical mirror and cup, because they could be operated only by a certain kind of man. Desiring to make his discoveries available to whoever could use them, the goldsmith journeyed far and wide, seeking a recipient for the magic treasures.

At last he found an engraver of Bokhara with the necessary characteristics. To him he gave the objects, saying:

'Make good use of these. I shall return one day to see if they have brought you fortune.'

The first time the engraver looked into the mirror he saw the goldsmith struggling in a whirlpool, about to drown. He threw a pebble into the magic cup, and soon saw that the goldsmith was saved.

The second time he looked into the mirror, the goldsmith was seen to be surrounded by dangerous and concealed enemies. By the use of the cup the engraver was able to dispel them.

The third time that he looked into the mirror he saw that all the goldsmith's friends, associates and family were in all manner of difficulties. Again, by the use of the cup, the engraver was able to effect their rescue.

When he looked into the mirror again, the engraver saw that he was himself threatened by difficulties. So he threw a pebble into the cup, and his problems vanished.

Many months later, when the goldsmith returned, he found his mirror and cup gathering dust on the engraver's bench, and the engraver still working away at the fine work which was ruining his eyesight.

He was incensed.

'I have been to so much trouble making these magical objects. Then I had to find a fitting recipient for them,' he fumed, 'and yet you neglect them and put them aside as if they were nothing. You do not even use them to succour your friends! Why have you not made yourself rich?'

The engraver said nothing; for how could one reason with a man who, rare skills or not, jumped at conclusions without thought or due inquiry?

He picked up the magical cup and a pebble which lay beside it.

By this time the goldsmith had become so enraged that he was waving his arms threateningly and calling the engraver all sorts of names.

Fumbling a little with the objects, because of his poor eyesight, the engraver allowed the pebble to fall into the cup.

The Guardian of the Cup, seeing the goldsmith in a threatening posture, made him disappear: and he has never been seen since.

The Onion

THERE was a time and a country in which onions were rare, almost unknown.

Someone left a large onion standing in the public square of the principal town of that land.

The citizens, or many of them, were interested in this curious object. They could see that it was some kind of vegetable.

The first person to venture near it coughed by chance as he approached. He immediately went away to teach that 'onions cause coughs'.

The second found it had a strong smell. Although he wanted to take some of it, he said to himself:

'If the outside is as strong as this, then the inside must indeed be impossible to bear.'

So he left it alone.

The third man made a cut in the onion. One layer came off in his hand.

'Miraculous object,' he said to all and sundry. 'This has magical qualities. You cut it and it discards the whole of its outside, leaving an inside which is just the same!'

The fourth man stripped off another layer. He took it away, cooked and ate it. He found it delicious. Then he taught others to do the same.

'However many layers you bear away, this amazing vegetable always presents you with another: this is a kind of perpetual harvest,' they exclaimed.

Someone remarked:

'It seems to be getting smaller.'

'That is a sheer optical illusion,' said the others, because they wanted to believe that the onion was everlasting.

And when the last jacket had been ripped from the onion?
Everyone exclaimed:

'Undoubtedly a magical but yet a treacherous thing, this!
It can not only disappear, but does so without any warning
at all.'

They all agreed, as indeed was the most sensible thing to do,
that people were better off, on balance, without onions.

Time

SEVERAL people went to Simab and found him silent.

They went away, afterwards telling everyone whom they met that he was lazy and worthless.

Certain of Simab's disciples went to him and said:

'Your repute is suffering because you have not attended to those people as you do to us.'

Simab said:

'What would you have me do?'

They said:

'Give them something of what you give us.'

Simab said:

'The motive is honourable but the possibility is absent. Shall I give them what I give you instead? Do you want them to be served to the extent that you will leave me and let me attend to them? Or do you merely want them to be silenced, so that you will not feel uncomfortable in being called the disciples of an unworthy person?'

The Wand

IN some cultures, miracles are effected, in legend, by waving fairies' wands. In others, there is the spirit of the magic ring. The objects vary: sometimes they are swords, for instance, sometimes cups. They originate from strange supernatural creatures, variously named.

People have always been curious about these objects, and have indeed sought them far and wide.

But why is it so difficult to find them? Why can one not seem to be able to make contact with the creatures who make or operate these wonders?

I shall tell you. You may even believe me.

Once upon a time, when this kind of story was first used, the sages who told them used to say clearly what the objects were, and who the creatures were.

But this information so conflicted with all human beings' imaginings about magical objects and powerful creatures, and so affronted them, that they turned upon the tellers, and many were killed.

Since then the identity of the creatures, and the real nature of the objects, has always been concealed well enough to prevent easy interpretation, and to cause the more destructive people to sneer at the whole idea as primitive, ridiculous, spurious.

'If you want your food to be safe from the greedy tell them that it is poisonous. Better still, let them suppose that they are clever enough to discover that it is harmful or useless to them.'

The Sun and the Lamps

SOMEONE said to Jan Fishan Khan:

'What we have heard of the Concealed Activity has been rumoured for centuries. But it is an extraordinary thought.'

'Why is it extraordinary to you?' asked the Khan.

'Because it postulates that, in spite of the thousands of visible centres of studies of the Sufis, nevertheless these are nothing compared to those places which we cannot recognize, because they do not have the appearance of shrines, tombs of saints or abodes of wisdom.'

Jan Fishan Khan said:

'It depends upon the viewpoint, and where you are looking. The visible places of Sufi study are like lamps in the dark. The inner places are like the Sun in the sky. The lamp illuminates an area for a time. The sun abolishes the dark.

'If you do not conceive of this you will naturally be surprised when you hear it. But the surprise is no greater than if you were night people who for some reason never ventured out of sleep during the day. The night people, knowing darkness, see lamps partly because darkness is present. To those who seek light, light itself is perceptible without darkness to display it.'

The Goat

THERE was once a country where goats were almost unknown. That is to say, everyone had heard of them, but so far no goat had ever been brought there.

Because of this, everyone was much attached to the idea and thought of goats.

The lack of real information about goats had not prevented the scholars of that land from collecting, sifting, comparing and enlarging upon whatever scraps of information there were about goats.

Those who, not unnaturally, became obsessed by goats, were known as 'the Believers'.

As a result of the intellectual and emotional life centering upon goat-study, everyone believed that there was a great deal of knowledge available about goats. Some were even sure that the last word on goats had been said.

One day a man crossed the border into this fascinating land. With him he brought – a goat.

'It is ours by right!' said the goat-worshipping priests.

'It is ours to study!' said the goatological scientists.

'It is ours to eat!' said others who could not think of any other claim to make.

The owner of the goat was amazed. He said:

'How can it be yours, for any purpose at all, when it is *mine*? If you are so excited about it, buy it from me and let me go.'

Someone shrilled:

'How could anyone *sell* anything as important and rare as a goat?'

It was decided, for this and other reasons, that the animal

was not a goat at all. This must mean, of course, that its owner was a fraud. It looked like what they had heard a goat looked like, but this must be spurious.

The scholars and jurists decided that the man must be punished, and he was put in prison.

The goat was placed on a platform, to test its supernatural qualities, and also to receive the respects of the populace.

Deprived of food it languished and died.

This proved that it could not be a real goat, and that it was useless to the people of that country.

The Imbecile Teacher

A CERTAIN Sufi received a young man who had many opinions but few experiences. When they had spoken for an hour or two, the other people present noticed that the Sufi was speaking more and more obtusely.

Presently the young man, unable to restrain himself, was calling the Sufi 'an imbecile'.

When this youth had gone on his way, several people begged the Sufi to explain the reason for his behaviour, but he simply smiled and said nothing.

Some even imagined that the Sufi was becoming so old that he had been unable to hold his own with the visitor.

One day, when an illustrative story was needed, the Sufi returned to the subject. He said:

'Some of you will remember that there was a day when a youth came here and I behaved like a stupid old man. The fact is that he was moved only by opinion and had no current ability to admit experience. It was beyond my power to cross the barrier raised by opinion. If I had tried to explain this to him, he would only have surmised that I wished to criticize him. He needed information, not knowledge (*malumat*, not *maarifat*).

'As a host, I had an obligation. The obligation of the host is to give the guest what he desires. The only service he would permit me was to bring out his hauteur and to increase the manifestation of his crudity to such an extent (regardless of my appearance) that he might be able to observe his own difficulties and abandon them.'

The Fool

THERE was once a man who did one thing right, and one thing wrong, in that order.

The first thing was to tell a fool that he was a fool.

The second thing was not to have made sure that he was not standing beside a deep well.

Transaction

SOMEONE said to Ardabili:

'The wonderful relating of the interchanges of masters and disciples serves to illuminate much in my heart. But there is one matter which is dark.'

'And what is that?' the Sufi asked.

'You relate the doings but not always the occasion. Sometimes you relate the occasion but not the name of the participants. Such omissions are far from the traditional scrupulous procedure of the men of letters.'

Ardabili said:

'Enchanting friend! If I were to display an angel, would you need to know its original home? If I were to teach you how to drink a goblet of water, would I have to say, "See – this is the manner of drinking of the Sultan of Khorasan!" Such questions have their own answers, except for the heedless.'

The Fish and the Water

A FISH is the worst source of information on water.

It does not know that water is there when it is present, and only becomes agitated by its absence.

Even when deprived of it, the fish does not know what his problem is – only that he feels bad, even desperate.

There is a fable about fish. They say that when a fish is scooped out of the water and lies gasping on the bank, he regards his misfortunes as stemming from anything and everything that he can think of. Sometimes he fights, sometimes he gives up. Sometimes he thinks that he should fight the trees, the grass, even the mud, as authors of his misfortunes. But it is only by accident that he ever flips back into the water. When he does he thinks how clever he has been. Generally, however, he dies.

Fish never see the net or know the hook. At best they blame the worm on the hook, the ropes to which the net is attached.

How sad to be a fish! How fortunate to be a man!

Mouseolatry

A MOUSE one day found his way to the Fountain of Knowledge. Whoever drinks from it may have his heart's desire – and one extra wish.

The mouse drank, and he wished that he could understand the speech of men, if men had speech.

When he had spent some time listening to what men said, he used his extra wish to banish his new power.

The other mice said to him:

'What was so horrible about the speech of men?'

At first he could not bring himself even to think of it again, but they pressed him so much that he said:

'I do not think that you will believe me, but what I have to say is true. Men actually imagine that God is like them, with human, not mouselike, attributes!'

The mouse audience was shocked to the core.

When some intellectuals among them had recovered from their indignation, they asked:

'But are there none who think otherwise?'

'There are some, but their theories are as abominable as the rest.'

'Tell us, just the same,' clamoured the thinkers, 'so that we may have the fullest information on this amazing matter.'

'Well, then; for instance there are those who imagine that religious terms are in reality derived from states of mind.'

'Enough!' cried some of the assembled mice, 'such insanity could cause an epidemic of madness. Even the Mouse-god might not be able to protect us from it.'

'Enough!' exclaimed others, 'for this might give mouseolaters a chance to revive that nonsense called religion, pretending that it has a functional origin.'

'I told you all at the beginning that it was horrible,' said the mouse who had found his way to the Fountain of Knowledge.

Six Lives in One

THERE was once a young man who thought:

'If I could only experience various phases of existence, I would be able to escape from narrow-mindedness. What is the use of being told: "You will know when you are old," when I shall be too old to do anything about it?'

He met a wise man who said, in answer to these questionings:

'You can find out the answer, if you will.'

'How?' asked the other.

'By multiple transformation. Eat certain berries which I will show you, and you can go forward and back in age, or go from being one "person" to being another.'

'But I don't believe in reincarnation.'

'It is not a question of what you believe, but of what is possible,' said the sage.

So he ate the berries, and desired to become middle-aged. But being of that age had so many limitations that he ate another, and found himself very old. Now that he was old, he wanted to be young again, so he ate another berry.

Now he was young again, but as every state has its corresponding degree of knowledge, the experience which he had gained in his two transformations fell away from him.

But the young man still remembered the berries. Now he determined upon a second experiment. He ate another berry, this time wishing to become 'someone else'. No sooner did he find himself transformed into that person than he realized that change by itself was useless. So he ate another berry and desired to die and to return as himself again.

This time, when he found himself restored to his original state, he realized that all that remained with him, anything of any value, was quite different from the 'experiences' which he had so prized in the past as indicative of a change in himself.

The sage appeared before him again. He said:

'Now that you know that it is not the experiences that you *want*, but the ones which you *need* which are significant– you can perhaps start to learn.'

Opposition

A MAN named Imami, who was notorious for his almost unbearable criticisms of others, arrived to visit a Sufi teacher one day.

'I have dedicated my life to opposing those whose beliefs are untrue, and to struggling against those who preach errors,' he said, 'and I am generally able to cause them to cry out for mercy, such is the power of my rightful attacks.'

The Sufi said:

'Have you put yourself in their place before doing this?'

'Yes, indeed,' said Imami, 'I have done so in order to attack them the better, as well as to realize their weaknesses.'

At this the Sufi started to vituperate. He shouted and raged and called the luckless Imami every adverse thing under the sun. Imami broke down and begged the Sufi to stop.

The Sufi said:

'I said what I did so that you could really *feel* what your opponents feel when they are being assailed. You say that you have put yourself in their place. But I see that when *I* put you in their place, you really start to feel it.'

Scientific Advance

A MOTH was fluttering outside a window, having seen a light in a room beyond it.

A spider said to it:

'When will you moths learn that flames are hot and destructive? You are annoyed at the presence of the glass. But it is the glass which saves you from destruction.'

The moth laughed. 'Grandad,' it said, 'there are two answers to you. First, you are an insect-eater and your advice to insects, however true, can never be accepted by them.

'Second, we moths of the present generation know more than you think. I happen to know that the delicious light in that room is cold light. There have been scientific developments since your time, you know.

'I shall enter through this chink and snuggle up to the light.'

So saying, the moth struggled into the room.

There was nobody there to stop him. No spider had made a web which might be a hazard.

The moth fluttered around the cold light in an ecstatic dance.

But scientific advances had indeed taken place.

The light was protected by a film of D.D.T.

Service

BABA MUSA-IMRAN lived the life of a rich merchant, although his sayings were accepted as those of a saint. People who had studied with him were to be found as teachers in places as far apart as China, it was said, and Morocco.

A certain man of Iran, assuming the garb of a dervish wanderer, found the Baba's home after much searching. He was received kindly and assigned the work of keeping the garden's irrigation channels clear. He stayed there for three years, without receiving any instruction in the mysteries. At the end of this time, he asked a fellow-gardener:

'Can you tell me if I may expect to be admitted to the Path, and how much longer I might have to wait? Is there anything which I should do, in order to qualify for the *Iltifat*, the kindly attention, of the Master?'

The other man, whose name was Hamid, said:

'I can only say that Baba Musa has assigned us tasks. Performing a task is a period of Service, known as the Stage of Khidmat. A disciple may not move out of the stage assigned to him. To do so is to reject the teaching. To seek something else or something more may be an indication that one has not, in reality, even been properly in the Stage of Service.'

Less than a year later, the Iranian gardener asked permission to leave, to seek his destiny.

Another thirty years passed and this same man one day found himself in the presence of his former companion, Hamid, who was now Murshid of Turkestan. When Hamid asked if there were any questions, the Iranian stood up and said:

'I am your former fellow-pupil from the Court of Baba Musa-Imran. I quitted the studies in the phase of *Khidmat*,

Service, because its relevance to the Teaching was incomprehensible to me. You, too, at that time, were performing menial tasks and attending no lectures.

'Can you tell me the particular point at which you began to make progress in the Path?'

Hamid smiled and said:

'I persevered until I was truly able to exercise service. This only happened when I ceased to imagine that menial work was in itself enough to denote service. It was then that its relevance to the Path became comprehensible to me. Those people who left our Baba did so because they wanted to understand without being worthy of understanding. When a man wants to understand a situation when he only imagines that he is in it, he is sure to be at a loss. He is incapable of understanding, so desiring it is not enough. He is like a man who has placed his fingers in his ears and shouts "Talk to me!" '

The Iranian asked:

'And after you had perfected your Service, did the Baba confide the Teachings to you?'

Hamid said:

'As soon as I was able to serve, I was able to understand. What I understood resided in the surroundings prepared for us by the Baba. The place, the others there, the actions, could be read as if he had painted a picture of the mysterious realities in their own language.'

The Tristomachic Survival

ONCE upon a time there were three kinds of people on a certain planet. There were those with one stomach, those with two and those with three stomachs.

At first nobody realized that there was any difference between them. They lived in different areas, and adopted the food and habits which corresponded best with their stomachic peculiarities.

But as they multiplied their differences became matters of contention. Sometimes the monostomachics prevailed, sometimes the bistomachics, sometimes the tristomachics.

Then with realism and through a desire for equity, they decided to abolish all differences based on stomachs. The result was that people, happily enough, eventually forgot that there were any of these anatomical differences. They now had a unified culture, which was completely blind to this detail. Even the technological instruments devised by the people did not register stomach differences.

And then, a new element crept in. As food supplies increased in quantity and decreased in quality (for unforeseen reasons) the monostomachics and bistomachics could not endure the new diet and began to die out.

Because the ancient taboo against knowing anything about stomachs had been established even in the genetic inheritance of the people, nobody could solve the problem, and only the tristomachics survived.

Tiger

A DEER, in flight before a hunting tiger, paused long enough to call out to a mouse whom he saw sitting quietly beside his hole:

'The Lord of the Jungle approaches, the Tiger is in a killing mood, flee for your life!'

The mouse nibbled a piece of grass and said:

'If you had news of a marauding *cat*, that would be something which might interest *me!*'

Please do This

A CERTAIN Sufi was asked:

'How can you teach people to move in certain directions when they do not know your "language"?'

He said:

'There is a story which illustrates this. A Sufi was in a foreign country where the people knew only one phrase of his language. The phrase was: "Please do this."'

'He had no time to teach them more of his language. So, whenever he needed anything done, he had to demonstrate it, saying, "Please do this."'

'And in that way, everything *was* done.'

Sting

A CAT had cornered a scorpion, who decided to plead for his life:

'Spare me, spare me! You can catch plenty of other things with more reward than a mouthful of gristle. If you let me go, I'll tell you my secret.'

Curious like all cats the cat leant forward and the scorpion whispered into his ear.

The scorpion was allowed to go, and the cat went back to his master.

As soon as the man picked him up, the cat, with his new-found skill, buried his claws with a backwards movement in his master's arm. No scorpion could have done better.

And the man put the cat in a bag and dropped the bag into a river.

Contradictions

An interchange between a Sufi and an enquirer:

'Which statement should one choose if two Sufi sayings contradict each other?'

'They only contradict one another if viewed separately. If you clap your hands and observe only the movement of the hands, they appear to oppose one another. You have not seen what is happening.

'The purpose of the "opposition" of the palms was, of course, to produce the handclap.'

The Fruit

THERE were once three men, all of whom wanted fruit, though none of them had ever seen any, since it was rare in their country.

It so happened that they all travelled in search of this almost unknown thing called fruit. And it also happened that, at about the same time, each one found his way to a fruit tree.

The first man was a heedless man. He got to the tree, but had spent so much time thinking about the directions that he failed to recognize the fruit. His journey was wasted.

The second man was a fool, who took things very literally. When he saw that all the fruit on the tree was past its best, he said:

'Well, I've seen fruit, and I don't like rotten things, so that is the end of fruit as far as I am concerned.' He went on his way, and his journey was wasted.

The third man was wise. He picked up some of the fruit and examined it. After some thought, and racking his brains to remember all the possibilities about this uneatable delicacy, he found that inside each fruit there was a stone.

Once he knew that this stone was a seed, all he had to do was to plant, and tend the growth, and wait for – fruit.

The Slave Sufi

It is related that one of the Sufi great ones was a slave: Ayaz, who became the trusted companion of Sultan Mahmud of Ghazna.

A courtier, so runs the tale, said to him:

'You were a dervish and then carried into captivity. Then you served Mahmud for years, and you still do so. Such is your sanctity, however, that the Sultan would immediately give you your freedom if you asked for it. Why do you remain in this strange position?'

Ayaz heaved a deep sigh and said:

'If I cease to be a slave, where on earth is the man whom people will be able to point out as a slave who is a teacher? And, if I leave the King, who will be left to bring admonitions to courtiers? They will listen to me because I have the ear of Mahmud. It is you, dear friend, who made this little world like this for yourselves. And yet it is you who ask me why I am like this within this cage of men.'

Unlikely Legend

'COSMETIC Surgery,' said an eagle, 'is not only useful, it is practically a necessity, with the present development of the social environment.'

When he had his talons trimmed and his beak shortened, everyone liked the effect so much that they had it done, too.

Almost all of them, that is. The ones who did not trouble themselves about improving their appearance were the crows. *They* grew their claws, and waited for a day when the other predators should have practised chiropody and developed civilization for so long that they wouldn't know what to do with claws even if their social taboos, under pressure, allowed them to grow them again.

Surroundings

A CERTAIN Sufi called another man, who greatly respected him, to come and live in his house. But within four days, the Sufi left on a long journey, and was away for three years.

The guest felt extremely uncomfortable: deprived of his master's presence he was confused; and he even found himself looking after the affairs of the house.

Many years later, someone to whom he had confided his agitation returned to find that he had succeeded the Sufi, and his feelings were quite different now.

He said:

'What had seemed clear to me when I first arrived at my master's house was, I now see, really obscure. If he had stayed, I would not have been able to endure the intensity of his presence. As it was, what I wanted was to be with him. What I really *needed* was to breathe the air of his surroundings.'

The Outline

THERE was once a house beside which a climbing plant rooted itself in the ground.

As the years passed, the creeper covered the walls, leaving only a blurred outline to indicate that there was anything behind the greenery.

It became more and more difficult to get into and out of the house, through the ever-thickening greenery.

The house ceased to be used at all. When parts of it crumbled, even the outline changed.

When the house collapsed completely, it became a pleasing creeper-covered mound, about whose origin people only occasionally and idly wondered.

The creeper was the most concerned. It said:

'What an ungrateful edifice! I held it up for many years, but it threw itself on the ground just the same.' So it spread itself all over the surrounding countryside.

The Difference

AFTER giving a lecture, Sufi Putsirr asked whether there was anyone present who wanted to ask a question.

A visitor said:

'I have heard a great deal about the wonderful qualities of the Master Inabi of Balkh. But when I visited him I found him attended by only a handful of people, and what is more, he did not speak to any of them, sometimes for months on end. There were people there who told me that he had never addressed a single word to them. I come here and find you so much more lucid, and so numerously attended, that I am forced to conclude that it is you whom I should respect.'

Someone objected that this was not a question, but a statement.

The master said:

'This is in fact a question, though it is not specifically put as one. But it is more clearly a question than the majority of questions, which are generally challenges or statements. So let us treat it as a question.

'Master Inabi has few people around him because he has been famous for forty years. During that time all sensationalists and lost dogs have visited him and discovered that he is a teacher and not an entertainer, and they have gone on their way. But, since I have been here only about twelve years, I am still surrounded by many who, whatever their outward appearance, are greedy for knowledge and anxious for excitement. Had you not noticed that there are always more sheep in any given place than there are lions in their own place?'

The Crystal

THERE is a legend which tells of a young man's search for knowledge through experience. He followed everyone and practiced everything that he could think of, to seek what there might be for man beyond the dimensions of ordinary life.

Eventually he arrived at the cave of a very ancient sage, who sat with a crystal in front of him. The young man seated himself before the sage and gazed into the shining surface.

He saw all kinds of things which he had never even heard of, and things which he had never even imagined. Then he said to the master:

'It is not enough to be a spectator, even to these wonders. I must somehow manage to live through them.'

The sage invited him to step into the crystal. As soon as he tried, the young man found that he could, indeed, walk into any of the scenes which he had witnessed.

Presently he stepped out of the crystal again. Without a word the sage handed him a hammer, and the young man smashed the ball to fragments and walked away.

Selfishness

WHEN asked why he did not criticize people, Anwar, son of Hayyat, said:

'Selfishness. If someone exposes a fault of a neighbour, it can be good for a village. But if he is not a man who has overcome arrogance, he will make himself more arrogant by exercising criticism.

'I am too selfish to want to be contaminated by deepening my arrogance.'

Experience

A CERTAIN Sufi was asked:

'Why did you travel so much in your youth, gaining such a variety of experiences?'

He answered:

'Because if I had done it once I was well known, people would have treated me differently, and so I would not have had the experiences.'

The Botanists:
Land without Medicine

ONCE upon a time, many years ago, there was a garden, tended by loving and talented workers. The garden was developed, through effort and sacrifice, from waste land; and at a time when nobody in the whole world cared about gardens. The botanists and other specialists who worked here over a vast expanse of time sent out expeditions to find and bring back every kind of plant from the most remote places imaginable.

Some of the plants, like cotton, yielded fibres suitable for spinning. Others provided nutritious food. Other plants, again, had medicinal virtues.

But then a calamity struck the garden, so that most of the gardeners were killed. The remainder of them were compelled to withdraw to distant places. In due course, other people arrived. They soon recognized the practical value of food-plants, and they cultivated them. Then they discovered that some of the flowers and herbs could be used as dyes. Finally, for they were indefatigable experimenters, they penetrated the secrets of the textiles which could be made from fibrous material.

And yet, strangely, these people failed to discover the special properties of the medicinal plants: and so they had no real medical science at all. When they became ill, they spoke incantations; and they either recovered, or were maimed – or died. This they regarded as the right and natural order of events. Some legends about medicine reached them from time to time; but they were a rational people and did not believe in this 'cult', since it sounded like a superstition or wishful thinking – as it would to you if you had been brought up without it. They said:

'Of course, everyone wants to become better, so people have fantasized the "science of medicine".'

The botanists, however, still existed. Some of them came back to the place which had formerly been their garden, planted by their own ancestors. It was then that they discovered, to their dismay, that medicine was now regarded locally as archaic nonsense. 'We should soon be able to put people right on this,' they said, 'for we can demonstrate that illnesses can be cured, in many cases, by simple means, through an expert knowledge of plants.'

They were, to be sure, not only botanists but also people of caution. Before attempting to restore the knowledge of leech-craft, they carried out a survey of the nature and behaviour, the thoughts and the institutions, of the people who now lived in the garden.

It was then that they received a shock. The people who had superseded them were (apart from a minority generally totally unsuited for the study of medicine) overlaid with such habits of selective reasoning that even demonstration would not convince them that there could be such a thing as medicine. True, they clamoured for demonstration; but then they would not allow the scientists – the Anachronists, as they called them – to demonstrate medicine in a manner which would allow a cure to take place. For instance, they insisted upon their own conditions: such as that all cures should take place within six minutes, or that nothing should be taken internally as a medicine, in case it harmed someone.

So the scientists went into seclusion again, until the people should become so desperate and so riddled with disease that they would submit to the 'superstitious' treatments which they otherwise shunned. Or until there were enough dispassionate students among those who reckoned that medicine was a possibility for real demonstrations to be held.

Worse

A PHILOSOPHER said:

'Such a great deal of conversation among dervishes is concerned with the "refining of man". I am tired of this; for, as an objective man, I want to hear the other side – about making man worse!'

A dervish who was present said:

'Felicitous one! Talking about man being better or about his being worse serves both purposes. Among those who have not got the basis, there is no quicker way to make a man worse than to talk about his "refinement". Why else would dervishes decline to teach all comers?'

Money

THERE is a story about a man who went to a dictionary-compiler and asked him why he was interested in money. The lexicographer was quite surprised and said, 'Wherever did you get that idea?'

'From your own writings,' said the visitor.

'But I have only written that one dictionary – that is my writings,' said the author. 'I know, and that is the book which I have read,' said the other man.

'But the book contains a hundred thousand words! And out of those, I don't suppose that more than twenty or thirty are about money.'

'What are you talking about all the other words for,' said the visitor, 'when *I* was asking you about the words for *money*?'

Evaluate

'ALWAYS evaluate evidence critically,' said a wise man of the Land of Fools to one of his students.

'Now I shall test you on feasibility. Suppose I were to say: "Climb up that moonbeam", what would you answer?'

'I would say: "I might slip on the way up".'

'Wrong! You should have thought of chopping footholds with an axe.'

In Due Season

'WHY', a visiting cleric asked Jan Fishan Khan, 'do critics and detractors make more noise than those who value the Path?'

'You can answer the question yourself,' said the Khan, 'if you find the answer to this:

'A shouting boy is throwing stones at a tree. People stop and watch him. A wise man passes by and notes that the tree is one which bears delicious fruit. The boy is completely absorbed in his amusement. The onlookers are looking only at what the boy is doing. The wise man is seeing the inwardness of the tree, which will only be manifested for the others in its due season.'

Radios

I WAS once in a certain country where the local people had never heard the sounds emitted from a radio receiver. A transistorized set was being brought to me; and while waiting for it to arrive I tried to describe it to them. The general effect was that the description fascinated some and infuriated others. A minority became irrationally hostile about radios.

When I finally demonstrated the set, the people could not tell the difference between the voice from the loudspeaker and someone nearby. Finally, like us, they managed to develop the necessary discrimination of ear, such as we have.

And, when I questioned them afterwards, all swore that what they had imagined from descriptions of radios, however painstaking, did not correspond with the reality.

The Young Sufi

An old man visited a young Sufi, sitting among a group of friends. The other visitors were scornful when he said:

'All my life I have hoarded money, and I have spent no time in reflecting upon man and his inner reality.'

The Sufi said:

'Each man does, with what he has, what he can.'

'Yes,' said the ancient miser, 'and, since I do not know any other way to honour you, whom I now recognize, I give you this. It is a gem which I bought at the goldsmith's. I paid for it every penny which I have saved these past sixty years. It is the best thing he had in his shop. *I* am too old to change, but each man speaks in his own language.'

The young Sufi stood up and started to rend his clothes. He said to the assembled company:

'You are thinking that this man is materialistic, and lacks knowledge. But he is parting with the most precious thing he has, because of *his* nobility of spirit, not mine! From this day on, this man is your teacher, and I shall go into seclusion.'

The Magical Book

ONE day an English historian discovered among some books which he had bought one which dealt with magical spells.

He put the book aside, but one day he thought:

'Magic is absolute nonsense, but wouldn't it be remarkable if a historian, from the best possible motives, could make use of the spells to project himself into the past, he would be able to learn the real facts of history ... '

And so it was that our historian found himself in Britain during the Norman conquest. When he had lived there for a time, he pronounced the magic word for returning to his own time.

Not long afterwards, he gave a lecture on Britain in Norman times. He was soon deprived of his university post because he insisted upon 'making allegedly factual claims without citing his literary sources, and alleging that all the historically-established facts about Norman Britain were incorrect.'

His library was sold up, and the book of magic found its way to the Middle East.

It was bought by a man named Mansour, who was as attracted as the English historian by the space-time formula. He projected himself back to the taking of Constantinople by Mohammed the Conqueror, just as a matter of interest.

Since in his community the practice of magic was considered to be undesirable, he told nobody about his adventures.

But, being only human, he could not resist using his new information. One day he said:

'It strikes me as curious that the Moslems wear the fez as a headgear indicating their religion, when it was formerly worn only by Christians in Byzantium. And, as for the crescent-and-star emblem, it was used by the Christians whom the Moslems were fighting.'

The ecclesiastical authorities in his country declared him a heretic, and nobody would talk to him until he retracted every word; which he soon did.

He threw the book out of his window, and it was picked up by a beggar, who sold it for a scrap of bread to the owner of a bookstall.

The book was written in English, and a foreigner who knew the language bought it for next to nothing on his way back to the West.

This man, whom we shall call Martin, became fascinated by the very same passage in the book as had interested his predecessors. But, being a good Catholic, he took it to a Cardinal of his acquaintance, and asked him about it.

The Cardinal said:

'My son, this is a grievous sin, and such an object as this is an abomination to all believers. Shun it!'

Martin was appropriately grateful for this guidance, and he left the book with the Cardinal.

Some time later, sitting in his study, the Cardinal pondered:

'After all, a man of my position is well able to defend himself against supernatural forces. I can see the dangers in sending oneself backwards to a time where things are not what they seem to us to be from where we are now. I will therefore, as an experiment, make up a special formula.'

After a great deal of thought, he recited the spell to take him back in time and space, like this:

'Let me be projected back to a time and to a place where things will not interfere with my beliefs.'

He closed his eyes, and when he opened them again, he found that he was in a cave. He heard sounds like those made by people, just outside. Adjusting his gorgeous robes, the cardinal stepped to the entrance of the cave. Assembled in a small hollow in front of him were a few dozen men and women, clad in skins, holding clubs and with long matted hair. They grunted as he appeared, and gave out shrill cries, apparently of welcome.

'Friends,' said the Cardinal, 'I do not know where I am, but I can see that you are in need of guidance. I have come to speak to you of the most important thing that you have ever heard.'

But all he could elicit by way of a reaction was grunts and squeals. By the time that he realized that he had journeyed back several hundred thousand years, he also found that he had forgotten the word which had to be pronounced in order to return him to his own time.

The book has now been sold and has started on its travels again, and now lies on the shelf of a second-hand dealer, awaiting its next buyer. It is just as well for most people that almost everyone regards such books as nonsense ...

The Man

A BEKTASHI dervish approached a certain bishop and said:
'I have heard of a young man who harangues crowds,
advocating their breaking the law, claims supernatural con-
nections, performs "miracles" and contradicts himself...'

'Enough!' said the bishop. 'He shall be tried, charged with
blasphemy and upsetting public order. If he does not recant,
he may be put to death as a heretic and corrupter. Just tell
me his name, and I shall arrange the rest!'

'I wish you could realize how impressed I am by your
competence,' said the Bektashi. 'His name is Jesus.'

Psychoanthropological Report

THERE is a country where all the people are eccentric for part of the time. They are not at all like the human beings whom we know.

They train groups of people to behave in certain systematic manners. When this has been done, they elicit that behaviour and all its surrounding actions, by applying the necessary stimuli.

Those people who show the greatest efficiency in training, the best indoctrination subjects, are given rewards, just as are laboratory animals who successfully reproduce their conditioning plan.

But at this point, unlike us, these people become quite confused, in the most systematic manner: the trainers themselves, instead of saying, 'Another experiment successfully completed,' start to admire and worship the 'heroes'. They set them up as inspirers, actually claiming that what they did was 'spontaneous'.

The result is that anything really spontaneous is punished and disliked, and cannot survive in their society. But as they have the word left over, they use it for non-spontaneous things.

This is all such a pity, since they are at times very pleasant people to be with, having far greater capacities than this self-deceptive one. And theirs is, to many visitors, a beautiful country. Because of the drawback just described, of course, most people who do not have to go there avoid it. They become irritated, noting that the citizenry of this place actually have scientists who carry out clinical and experimental work on animals and humans without noting similar effects in everyday society. This they claim is the experimenting and conditioning. But what they do among themselves, something precisely the same, after laboratory hours, that is not.

But are the results of the scientists' indoctrination processes secret? Good gracious, no! They are printed by the million in popular books, and very widely read.

We *are* lucky to live in our kind of world.

Frivolous

A PRINCE said to a scholar:

'The speech of yonder Sufi is so frivolous and so general that I do not believe that he can be a man of sincerity.'

The scholar said:

'O Emir of Sheikhs! Know that there are three forms of deep knowledge:

The Deep Knowledge unknown to any;

The Deep Knowledge given by the results of complex speech;

and the Deep Knowledge conveyed by seemingly frivolous means.

One jest from the lips of that Sufi has made a hundred saints; while other men, of serious mien and threatening talk, have succeeded – in making corpses.'

A goblet of the Water of Life was once handed to a man
He refused to drink because the container did not please him
    by its outward shape
If you are a man of 'shape', why do you talk about 'depth'?

Stop Og Now . . .

So the great 'discovery' has come at last. The arch-rebel, blasphemer, jack-of-all-trades called Og has essayed a new attention-attracting move. His last wonderful piece of advice, it will be remembered, was 'Carry five things at once; instead of making several journeys, make one.' The priesthood, as any intelligent man could have foreseen, soon put an end to that; and of course it was only a matter of time before Og came up with something else. If the Great Totem had intended us to behave like children, to fill our arms with objects in fumbling disarray, it would have been laid down in the Magical Chants. We *know* (as the Great Chief Hoodoo so sagely ruled) that it is more dignified, more apposite, more *right* to carry one thing at a time.

But we are becoming accustomed to Og. 'Innovator' he may call himself. But what innovation is there (even assuming the far from established thesis that innovation is good, for there is evidence to the contrary) in the mere repetition, under another guise, of rebellion and heresy?

Yesterday, as I have said, it was 'Carry more than one object at a time, and save time.' Today? The puerile pattern is repeated, though the undertones of challenge are more sinister. Today, friends, it is 'I can make fire without rubbing two sticks together.'

Formerly, of course, no decent man or woman would have allowed such an appalling sequence of words to pass his lips, even in order to refute them. But these are changed times, enlightened times, progressive times; stirring days which will ever be remembered as an age in which no forward-looking shaman, no truly thinking juju-man, flinched from facing evil and casting its very obscenities back into its foetid mouth.

Make fire by 'another method'? *Make fire at all*, without having been initiated by the Great Fetish in a ceremony of such sanctity that it can be performed only four times a year? Make fire any time you like'?

I would not blame you if your minds reeled at the very recital of this story. But it is not reeling minds, surely, which will mend the matter. No, it is cold logic, calm and effective thought, careful refutation on impeccable grounds.

Let us, therefore, calmly and logically, as well as from a very proper human conscience, examine these claims, outrageous and devoid of sense as they must surely appear to most of us.

The first consequence of the absurdity proposed would be that all beauty, all mystery, all that is fine in the basic sanctions of morality, would disappear from our lives. On fire, the rarity and sublimity of fire, for which lives have been given, for which people have suffered and for which many more are prepared to endure the greatest hardships, on the rarity and sublimity of fire, ultimately depend all higher values. What, in a word, is more sacred than fire?

What would become of the enchanting oath: 'May fire strike me from above if I lie?' Fire, instead of being respected, would soon come to be despised. No longer afraid of fire, people would lie, would cheat, would kill.

If – stretching credulity to its limits and producing, as a purely hypothetical exercise, a nonsense situation – the warmth of fire were to be available to all, how could its nurturing aesthetic, its divinely benevolent mercy, be valued for its scarcity? Today, people *win and earn* the right to fire. They are given it, from the temples, as a reward. Those who are, rightly, denied it, are all around us, blue and chattering with cold, object-lessons to us all as they, as a punishment for evil, have a foretaste of the greater punishment beyond.

And here, dear friends, we may very well have uncovered the real, the astoundingly audacious, motivation of the evil Og. As the generations have passed, more and more people have, again I say rightly, been denied fire. Naturally they think of little else. And then Og appears. He says: 'I can gain power over the people by promises. What do they want? Fire. So I shall promise them fire!'

Do you not now see how, at one blow, Og can strike at the very roots of civilization? If he promises fire, the disaffected will do anything for him. If, indeed, he *can* make it, he destroys society; there would be nothing to live for or to die for. If he cannot make it, he can destroy, through his minions, the makers of divine fire any time he wishes, out of sheer excitement and fanaticism.

Og says that we are conservative, timid and hypocritical, as a society. Is it conservative to range ever further in search of wild bison? Is it timid to protect the finest feelings known to man? Is it hypocritical to say 'You are trying to undermine us and are not offering any alternative to what you take away?'

To turn fire into a slave instead of a master; to make it a matter of switching on and off – how can this be good, or lead anywhere at all?

No, my friends. I do not like Og. I do not like the way he talks. I do not like the way he looks. I do not think it any coincidence that his forbears came from a different tribe. I do not believe Og, or believe in anything that his supporters say about him.

Can you conceive a world in which Og and his kind 'use fire', setting the forests alight as if they were the lightning-god himself?

Do you want a community in which the most progressive elements in society are called cowards and play-actors, their values assailed, their objectives declared irrelevant – and, above all, by *Og* and his kind?

And, finally, in lighter vein, so that the utter absurdity of the whole matter may become apparent even to the most obtuse: is Og a second Glug the Great, that the whole world should listen to him?

Has Og taken any part in our own progressive activities, that we should trust him through knowing his opinions and beliefs? Is he respected by any person whose opinions *we* value?

No, Og is distinctly an enemy. And it is always the cleverest and most dangerous enemies who pose as benefactors.

Let, therefore, the call go out: "STOP OG NOW ... "

Five Thousand

A MAN said to the Keeper of the Gate of Aleppo:

'I have lived in the Khanqah, the retreat, of the Master of the Age, in Turkestan, for twenty years.'

The Keeper asked: 'What did you learn?'

'I do not know if I have learned anything,' said the other man. 'While I was there, people came and went. Some were dismissed, many were disappointed. Finally I came away.'

The Keeper said:

'There is a great Sufi living beside the Small Market. Perhaps he may give you advice.'

The man from Turkestan went to the Small Market, and when he saw the great Sufi he exclaimed:

'Are you an impostor? For you are none other than the man who – for twenty years – appeared regularly at the Khanqah, sowing doubts about my Master in my mind!'

The Sufi smiled and said:

'One of my duties is to test disciples. What better way of testing than to be one of them, grumbling and illustrating their own coarseness?'

'But what of the others at that Khanqah? Were all my fellow-disciples really saints in disguise?'

'The composition of a Khanqah's population is such that there are some ignorant ones, some enlightened ones behaving like the ignorant, and others who are neither.

'You only see the superficial. In your two decades at the Khanqah, five thousand of the people who made no noise, many of whom you did not even look at, or who seemed unimportant, received their own illumination.'

The Man and the Snail

A MAN once saw a snail sitting in a crevice, in a wall.

He called out:

'Hello, Snail!'

Believe it or not, that snail could speak, and it could hear, and it said:

'Hello, there. What are you?'

The man said:

'I am a human being.'

'Are you like us?' asked the snail.

'In a way, but there are a lot of things which we can do that you cannot.'

'Name them.'

'Well, for instance, you have eyes on stalks. We have stalks on the other end, called legs. We have feet on them. By moving the legs and feet, we can cover vast distances in no time at all.'

'That sounds quite extraordinary! Anything else?'

'Well, we have no shell. We don't need one.'

'No shell? I suppose it is possible . . . Anything else?'

'And we can communicate without words, without even being together. Our method is to take something like, say, a leaf, make a mark on it, called writing, and send it by another human being. Now, by what is called "reading", the person who receives it can know what the "writer" was thinking.'

The snail said:

'The trouble with you, as with all liars, is that you go too far. I have trapped you into over-reaching yourself by pretending to believe you. But if I further encourage you by not expressing the disbelief natural to all rational beings, I shall be a partner in your sinful lies.'

The Doorkeeper

A Sufi was asked:

'What are you doing? You do not let us, who want to learn from you, study books. You do not perform rituals; you refuse to answer questions; you take no heed of praise or blame.'

He said:

'I am a doorkeeper. The doorkeeper makes sure that the door is open when it should be open, and that it is shut when it has to be shut. He permits the entry of whatever or whoever should enter, and he denies entry to what must be excluded.

'If you want him to make a noise, to "bang the door", to create an effect, to wear rich or poor clothes, to hold out promises or to argue, to mime, to accept bribes or to discuss instead of working – you are not a person to have transactions with the keeper of a door.'

The Letter of Thanks

SHAH SHARIF SHAH returned from a banquet at the house of the Prime Minister of the time in the country of Roum.

He immediately sat down and dictated a letter to the finest calligrapher in the city, packed with fulsome compliments and sticky honorifics.

A visiting thinker said:

'O Sharif! If you send this letter to the Minister, he will either be revolted by your adulation – and never invite you to his table again – or else he will so fear people's opinion that he was influenced by your flattery as never to offer you a high post at Court.'

Sharif Shah smiled and said:

'You have judged him well, and your reputation as a philosopher is illuminated by your diagnosis. But your assessment of me seems to have become confused with your own ambitions for yourself. Know, therefore, that, being desirous of fewer, not more, banquets, and even less enamoured by the prospect of positions at Court, I have composed the letter which you have just heard.'

The Knife

AN idiot out on a walk saw something gleaming beside the road. Hoping that it was silver, he picked it up; but it was only a knife which someone had dropped.

'I'll throw you away for deceiving me like that, into the river, where you'll rust to death,' he shouted at it.

But this was a talking knife, and it tried to save its life by saying:

'Good Sir, why do you not keep me? I could be useful, to cut your bread!'

'Not likely!' said the idiot, 'for you could also be used by someone else, to cut my throat.'

The Elixir

ONE of the great Sufi teachers was asked:

'How is it possible to comprehend the teachings of the Masters, when so much of their behaviour is paradoxical and frequently so very ordinary?'

He answered:

'General rules and hypothetical approaches block the understanding as often as they assist it. But I shall tell you my own experience, for the records of experience are often the best.

'When I was a student, I approached the greatest Master of the Age, and said: "I can only behave like an animal – consent to help make me human." He nodded his head and I attended him at his house for two years, waiting for a sign of teaching. After this time I went to another wise man and asked him how I could approach my teacher to learn from him.

'The wise man said: "You seek an elixir, and I shall give you one. Take this colourless fluid and put a drop in your master's food once a day. At the same time make sure that you serve him and do everything which he says, not for the time being making any attempt to see meanings in his actions, or to trick him into conversations."

'I did as he said, and after a month I found that I was developing perceptions and understandings. I returned to the wise man and said: "Blessings upon you! The elixir is undoubtedly working, for I am progressing, and can now do things formerly impossible to me."

'He said: "And is that why you have come?"

'I said: "I have also come for a little more of the magical elixir, for the quantity which you gave me is exhausted."

'He at once smiled and answered: "You may now stop giving your teacher drops of inert water – the 'Elixir' – and continue with the special behaviour which I prescribed for you." '

The Lion

ONCE upon a time there was a lion. He had come into being to be a lion, and to pass on lion-experience to cubs and other lions.

But certain gnats and flies who surrounded him imagined that he was there for their amusement and for their use.

The lion, by shaking his head and swishing his tail, prevented the insects from living off him. Although they scattered when he made any movement, they never learned that they should leave him alone, and that by approaching him they were acting through habit and impulse, not reason or effectiveness.

One day the lion died. He provided a place of sport for insects, and some of them lived for quite a long time off his carcass.

The insects thought that they had won the battle, since the lion did not now oppose them. To them, he was their property. Indeed, thinking insects constructed a system of thought to explain what the lion really was, based on their experiences of the dead body.

Because the voice of the lion had been stilled by nature, they and those who heard them supposed that the insect version of the aims and value of lions was correct.

This is one reason why so many lions leave behind cubs. Over a sufficient period of time, you see, insects will learn not to trouble lions, and also to go to places where they can get food more easily, which is better suited to them than the carcass of a lion. For one thing, it takes too long for a lion to die, and his meat does not last forever.

So it is, too, with Sufi teachers plagued by petty scholastics.

The Certificate

A CERTAIN man had been studying with a Sufi master for several years, having been sent by means of a subscription raised from the citizens of his home town.

When the time came for him to return, the master handed him a certificate. On it was written:

'I certify that this man has fasted constantly, has suffered extraordinary privations, has performed wonders and should be respected in every way.'

The disciple said:

'Why should you issue such an untrue and misleading document?'

The master said:

'Sufis do not exist by outward show, nor by the possession of certificates. But you just try explaining *that* to people who have paid for outward show and certificates. The people who made it possible for you to come here would be the first to revile you and claim that you had wasted their money if they were not shown their own kind of evidence for your importance.'

Cheese for Choice

'I HAVE chosen', said the mouse, 'to like cheese. Such an important decision, needless to say, cannot be arrived at without a sufficient period of careful deliberation. One does not deny the immediate, indefinable aesthetic attraction of the substance. Yet this in itself is possible only to the more refined type of individual – as an example, the brutish fox lacks the sensitive discrimination even to approach cheese.

'Other factors in the choice are no less susceptible to rational analysis: which is, of course, as it should be.

'The attractive colour, suitable texture, adequate weight, interestingly different shapes, relatively numerous places of occurrence, reasonable ease of digestion, comparative abundance of variety in nutritional content, ready availability, considerable ease of transport, total absence of side-effects – these and a hundred other easily defined factors abundantly prove my good sense and deep insights, consciously exercised in the making of this wise and deliberate choice.'

Hidden Hand

THE Khan Jan Fishan Khan was at one time frequently preached against by a certain Mulla of Kandahar. He called for reports of the Mulla's sermons and studied them, but he said nothing publicly.

Several months after this incident a traveller arriving from Mazar, one Abdul-Qadir Beg, who wrote about it in his memoirs, said:

'You were until quite recently preached against by the Sifri Mulla, and now, I am told, he never refers to you at all. Have you changed your ways, or is this magic? What alchemy, what talisman, can you have used?'

Jan Fishan Khan, says Abdul-Qadir, answered:

'If you promise to tell nobody until the Mulla is no more, I shall confide in you.

'I studied his speeches and saw that he contradicted himself. For instance, he objected to my administrative activities on the grounds that I was called a mystic, and my Sufi activities on the grounds that I was called a Khan. So the remedy was simple.

'I arranged, anonymously and through a merchant friend at the City of the Cloak of the Prophet, that the Mulla be appointed Adviser to the Merchants of Kandahar. Since he has a real occupation now, he no longer has to busy himself with making a noise to attract attention.'

City of Storms

ONCE upon a time there was a city. It was very much like any other city, except that it was almost permanently enveloped in storms.

The people who lived in it loved their city. They had, of course, adjusted to its climate. Living amid storms meant that they did not notice thunder, lightning and rain most of the time.

If anyone pointed out the climate they thought that he was being rude or boring. After all, having storms was what life was like, wasn't it? Life went on like this for many centuries.

This would have been all very well, but for one thing: the people had not made a complete adaptation to a storm-climate. The result was that they were afraid, unsettled and frequently agitated.

Since they had never seen any other kind of place in living memory, cities or countries without storms belonged to folklore or the babblings of lunatics.

There were two tried recipes which caused them to forget, for a time, their tensions: to make changes and to obsess themselves with what they had. At any given moment in their history, some sections of the population would have their attention fixed on change, and others on possessions of some kind. The unhappy ones would only then be those who were doing neither.

Rain poured down, but nobody did anything about it because it was not a recognized problem. Wetness *was* a problem, but nobody connected it with rain. Lightning started fires, which were a problem, but these were regarded as individual events without a consistent cause.

You may think it remarkable that so many people knew so little for so long.

But then we tend to forget that, compared to present-day information, most people in history have known almost nothing about anything – and even contemporary knowledge is daily being modified – and even proved wrong.

People

I⊤ is related in the Book of Amu Daria that a former lawyer, a scholar-jurist, who had joined Bahaudin Naqshband, asked him:

'You know all about dogma and exegetics; you seem to know all about theory and about what is in books. How can you manage to have all this knowledge when it is not as well developed in academic scholars and in dogmatists?'

'Well,' said Bahaudin, 'I can only say that I learned much more about dogma from sources other than books and arguments, or even from lectures.'

'What could such sources be?'

'I learned about dogma and scholasticism by studying *people*.'

What to Shun

Two worthy citizens of the Land of Fools were talking together.

'Do you know', said the first, 'that whenever I read the multiplication tables my head starts to swim?'

'But this is amazing!' shouted the second, 'because the very same thing happens to me when I run any distance.'

Unable to see any common explanation for the two happenings, they took their experiences to the Very Wisest Man of the Land.

The Very Wisest Man said:

'It is obvious that both numbers and running were invented by an undesirable person, and his influence still subsists in them – therefore shun both!'

Posture

ANWAR ABBASI was a man of such regularity of habits that people said:

'The Sun may not rise, but Anwar will always be reliable.'

When this was reported to him one day, he began to become extremely erratic. Since nobody could fathom the reason, opinions were divided, but many concluded that Abbasi was in some way unwell.

Then, as suddenly as he had changed, he resumed his former behaviour. Someone asked him, as delicately as possible, the purpose of his behaviour.

He said:

'I am glad that you, at least, think that I have a reason. Remember, I have many students. If I do not test their faith in me by abandoning outward show, I shall be no better than a priest, or anyone else who is schooled to remain silent, or who is trained to make no sound. A priest is one who achieves his successes by outward appearance and by behaviour alone, though everyone attributes his accomplishments to other things. Look at the people who are affected by external behaviour, look at the people who have given rise to priests – if you want to know whether this is for the good of mankind.'

The Killer

As you will know, there are many kinds of bacteria. Some are useful: they help us to digest our food; others, which have no discernible function, are quite harmless. And some, of course, cause diseases.

One day a certain dangerous bug was suddenly attacked by another and killed. A harmless bacterium standing near cried out:

'Murderer! This germ had done no one any harm, and yet you foully murdered it!'

The killer said:

'If it had been allowed to live, to attack mankind, or even animals, it would have done great harm; it would have perhaps stimulated anti-bacterial action; it might have deprived us of our host tissue.'

The offended micro-organism sniffed:

'I have met your kind before. Pretending greater enlightenment you claim greater right to dispose of others. You arrogate to yourself licence in the name of knowledge. I have no doubt that you are planning to kill me next.'

'Pray direct your attention, through this instrument, at a whole caucus of your friends, actually attacking a human being whom *they* are planning to destroy in the name of the legality of a feast for all,' said the other.

'Do you think that I have nothing better to do', asked the offended idealist, 'than to obey your orders, and get myself trapped into a course of action which may lead to my own destruction?'

All that the high-minded theoretician has succeeded in doing, however, is to teach the 'destructive' bacteria to keep their own counsel. But neither party can really understand the other.

Magician

A CERTAIN Sufi took up quarters in a caravanserai near a populous village not far from Jalalabad, in Afghanistan.

The villagers made a habit of telling all comers about Sahir, the dangerous magician of the locality.

'He must be the most dangerous wizard in the whole world,' they said.

The Sufi called everyone from the surrounding countryside for a meeting a few days after he had heard this for the fiftieth time. He said:

'O people! Gossip and imagination enervate the mind. I will now illustrate to you how your own love of idle talk has caused you to misunderstand Sahir.

'You say that he must be the most dangerous wizard in all the world, do you not?'

'Yes,' the people answered, 'although, as a traveller, you may of course have heard of a worse one, we admit that.'

'Your magician, whether I have heard of a worse one or not, is obviously far less dangerous than at least one other category of magician.

'The worst magician in the world is much more likely to be the very one who would not frighten you at all.'

'But', clamoured the people, 'what kind of magician would *not* frighten us?'

'A successful one, a real one. *He* would have the power to do his will and yet appear to you to be an honourable man. It is only the magician who is powerless who has to make you fear him.'

Visitors' Information

TRAVELLERS arriving on this planet will be glad to know that there is an established system of locating information and definitions, helping to clear up perplexing problems.

The system is called Dictionaries.

Minor difficulties, it is true, have been observed.

One visitor, trying to understand this thing called humanity, found that, according to the dictionaries:

HUMAN means 'about man or mankind'; MAN means 'mankind' or 'a human being'; MANKIND means 'man or human being'.

But every minus has a plus. This visitor drew his own conclusions on what all this really meant. He based his behaviour upon it.

When people asked him what *he* was, he said:

'A CLERP.'

When (not finding it in their dictionaries) they asked him what *that* was, he said:

'It is a GLOMP.'

And it worked out as he had expected. One-third of the people thought that he was mad, though harmlessly so, and he had no trouble with them.

One-third thought that he was up to something and must be dishonest, and they each condemned or ignored him, so he had no real trouble with them.

The remainder thought he was a saint.

Since nobody knew who or what he really was, he was able to carry out his scientific work with very little interruption.

Cheetahs and Awarts

A CERTAIN man had read many books on the Sufi way and after some time said to himself:

'This reading is useless. I must find someone who can teach me by direct methods.'

So he presented himself before the man whom, he had been told, was the Master of the Age, generally known as Gilgun.

Gilgun received him in a kindly manner, asking why he had come without first writing to him.

'I am tired of reading and writing, I want something real,' said the student.

'Very well,' said Gilgun, 'I shall show you the relation of reality to comparative reality.'

He gave orders that a cheetah was to be brought into the room. When it appeared, he said:

'Why do you not fear this animal?'

The student said:

'I have read that cheetahs are harmless to humans.'

'Know', said Gilgun, 'that we had a man here the other day who did not have this information. When the cheetah came in he fled in alarm. It was a pity, because he was thus prevented from enjoying the advantages of cheetahs. So your reading has been of use to you, whether you are tired of it or not.'

Then Gilgun said:

'Have you ever read of the Awarts?'

'No,' said the other man, 'I have no idea what an "Awarts" might be.'

'Call the "Awarts",' said Gilgun.

At that moment a frightful apparition, shaped like a man but with coloured stripes and fearsome head, rushed into the room. The would-be disciple cowered in the corner, terrified.

'Let this man go, and do not let him come into my presence ever again,' instructed the Master of the Age, 'because although anxious for real experience, he is unable to discern that an "Awarts" is a name for a man with paint and a mask on him.'

Ant Research

It took a certain scholar a lifetime of experiment before he could communicate with an ant. The one which he eventually found was a very wise and very ancient insect; but, at the risk of causing it pain, the scholar said:

'Our species is immeasurably superior to yours. We study you, and yet you cannot even begin to observe us.'

The ant said:

'If you, poor man, only knew about yesterday, you would understand today – and also be prepared for tomorrow.'

The scholar confessed himself confused by such statements, so the ant continued:

'Millions of years ago, we ants worked out what was going to happen on this earth. We knew that your species would come and ruin almost everything. So we did the only thing open to intelligent beings with complete information. We destroyed the data and forbade the breeding of ants who would understand, organizing ourselves in special colonies.

'Now and again we have a throwback – an ant who can see our miserable and irreversible fate. But untold myriads of heedless ants are happy; and will be so, until our time comes.

'That is the solution for ants. You humans, on the other hand, you have not even reached the stage when you know what may happen to you; and whether or not there is anything you can do about it.'

Duty

A CERTAIN Sufi was asked:

'People come for companionship, discourses and teaching. Yet you plunge them into activity. Why is this?'

He said:

'Though they – and you – may believe that they come for enlightenment, they mainly desire engagement in something. I give them engagement, so that they shall realize the limitations of engagement as a means of learning.

'Those who become totally engaged are they who sought only engagement, and who could not profit by self-observation of themselves so uselessly engaged. It is, therefore, not the deep respecters of activity who become illuminated.'

The questioner said:

'Who, then, is it who does become illuminated?'

The Sufi replied:

'The illuminated are those who perform duties adequately, realizing that there is something beyond.'

'But how is that "something beyond" to be reached?'

'It is always reached by those who perform adequately. They need no further instruction. If you were doing your duty adequately, and were neither neglectful nor fanatically attached to it, you would not have had to ask the question.'

The Right Man

A GENERAL riding across country became separated from his staff and eventually arrived at a small village, completely lost.

The villagers gathered around him, and he started to give them orders. He asked them to feed his horse, but they did not react at all. He called for a stable, for water, for blankets, and nobody moved.

'If you do not obey me instantly,' shouted the general, 'I shall act against you with the utmost rigour.'

The chief of the village said: 'You don't look very strong to me – how would you do anything to us, how could you?'

'It is not a matter of *my* doing anything,' shouted the infuriated general, 'it is a matter of the Chain of Command.'

'And what is the Chain of Command?'

'Well, I tell the colonel, and he tells the major, and he tells the captain, and he tells the lieutenant, and he tells the sergeant, who brings a squad of men. They stand you up against a wall and shoot you, puff, like that!'

'Now you are getting somewhere,' said the chief of the village, 'this sergeant, he really must be a powerful man. So far we've seen only you. But if we'd had the sergeant to deal with, from the beginning, *that* would have been something.'

Burdens

THREE dervishes were asked why they opposed a certain cleric who was full of technical terms and constantly spouted involved speculations and interpretations.

'He drags the whole body of the matter to the feast, sure enough,' said the First Dervish, 'but who eats a whole dead body without risk?'

'He is like the man in the fable. Too afraid not to "Watch the door" as ordered, he carried it on his back – and thieves broke into the house,' said the Second Dervish.

'Because he is greedy for knowledge, he is afraid of other people getting any. This is a burden which makes him unhappy,' said the Third Dervish. 'If he is unhappy, he makes other people anxious.'

The Wisest Tiger

A MAN spent years of his life learning the language of tigers. Then he made careful inquiries, to find the wisest of all tigers, because the ones he spoke to were generally, to his mind, not very clever.

When he managed to see the Wisest Tiger, he decided to put a few questions. 'What is mud?' he asked.

'Mud', said the Wisest Tiger, 'coats your feet and tickles when it gets dry.'

'And what happens in bushes?'

'We use them for concealment. Sometimes, too, they get in the way of one's whiskers.'

'What is man's greatest disability?'

'Having no claws.'

The man decided that tigers are uninteresting, and went on his way, rather crestfallen.

Soon afterwards a cheetah came up to the Tiger. 'What was that man doing, talking to you?' it asked.

'Oh, only some stupid fellow,' said the Wisest Tiger, 'who talked such trivia that I treated him like a simpleton.'

The Wrong Department

A STUDENT interrupted a Sufi who was reciting illustrative tales of the masters of the past, and said:

'I intervene at this point because I need information and ask you to indulge this need, even though it may be against the behaviour of the assembly and even conflicts with the conduct required of audition.'

The Sufi said:

'We are ready to hear you, even though something raised in this manner is unlikely to be of benefit to you or to us. If, however, your need is for interrupting, interrupt us.'

The student thanked the Sufi and continued:

'My question is that we are constantly hearing about the perfection of the attributes of the masters of the past and illustrations of the wisdom and excellence of the Sufis. May we not hear something of their shortcomings and occasions when they were not able to attain that which they desired, so that some kind of a balance might be struck in the matter?'

The Sufi said:

'Greengrocers do not stock rotten apples, they throw them away. People who apply to a doctor to see his dead patients have to be sent to a graveyard. If you wish to inspect the dustbins of this world, you will have to find some scavenger to direct you to them; and we do not always learn about straight lines by looking at crooked ones – because the world is already full of crooked lines; the student has only to try to draw a straight line to find that such materials are already there – within himself.

'Your question is one of the oldest in the world. It was in answer to it that the formula was first provided: "If you want to see a crooked line – do not look for a ruler." '

Expectations

One of the most eminent Sheikhs said:

'I used always to cause severe disappointment in everyone who came to me to become a disciple. I failed to appear at the appointed lecture times. I was lazy and forgetful. When I had promised to demonstrate an exercise or impart a secret, I usually did not do so at all.

'Now, first examine the effect if I had fulfilled the expectations of the disciple. He would have become so pleased with himself at having been given something that others lacked, that this pleasure would have inflated his pride.

'Only by experiencing disappointment can a person register its effects on himself. Disappointment cannot exist without expectation. No expectation in the Sufi Way is accurate. "The expected apricot is never as sweet when it reaches the mouth." '

Personal Wisdom

'I DON'T want to be a man,' said a snake.

'If I were a man, who would hoard nuts for me?' asked the squirrel.

'People', said the rat, 'have such weak teeth that they can hardly do *any* gnawing!'

'And as for speed ... ' said a donkey, 'they can't run at all, in comparison to me.'

How can it Mean Anything?

A GROUP of merchants asked a certain disciple:
   'How can this Sufi nonsense mean anything to you?'
He said:
   'Because it means everything to those whom I respect.'

Economics

A MAN saw his bus going so slowly that he decided to walk home.

On the way he met another man – a citizen of the Land of Fools.

'Ah, Foolslander!' he cried, 'I'm saving a shilling by walking instead of travelling in that bus.'

'You're a wasteful idiot,' the Foolslander immediately replied.

'Why?'

'Having discovered such an important saving as that, you could have walked behind a taxi, and saved ten times as much!'

Two Pilgrims

Two pilgrims were talking. The first one said:

'I have just been to the house of the great Sufi of such-and-such a place.'

'How did you know how to find it, and how did you know that he was a man of greatness?' asked the other.

'I was reliably informed that all his followers eventually became Complete Men, that even his anger was a benediction, and that he could rise into the air miraculously. And that his house was marked by a cypress tree in front of it.'

'And', asked the second pilgrim, 'did you find him to be as had been described?'

'No.'

'What happened?'

'When I reached the house I saw that the tree had died. So I said to myself: "He who does not learn from signs is a fool. Why waste any more effort?" And so I started on my travels again.'

Service

'How', said a seeker to a well-known Sufi, 'can one do even the minimum service towards helping the Teaching?'

'You have already done it,' he said, 'for to ask how to serve is already a contribution towards service.'

The Boy and the Wolf

I DREAMT that I was having a conversation with a Wolf. I said:

'You wolves are famous among us humans, and we have a lot of stories about you.'

The Wolf said:

'How interesting. What kind of stories?' So I told him the fable of 'The Boy who Cried Wolf!'

'That's funny,' said the Wolf, 'we haven't got *that* story. But there is one with the same two main characters. It is called "The Wolf who Cried Boy!" – but you must have heard it.'

'I'm afraid I haven't,' I said, and so the Wolf told it:

'Once upon a time there was a wolf. He got to know a boy who was also a wolf-hunter. As soon as he realized the danger of a human who was a hunter, the wolf ran from one pack of his brethren to another, shouting "Boy! Boy!"

'But, since the wolves had no idea what a boy was, and had little conception of wolf-hunters, they took no notice at all. And some of us say that it is because wolves are so silly, on the whole, that people – even boys sometimes – can hunt them.'

'But surely,' I said, 'if you have a fable like that, it will serve to warn all wolves that there *are* such dangers, and make them more careful?'

'I can see', said the Wolf, 'that some of you humans are not much more intelligent than the run-of-the-mill wolf. Like us, you seem to imagine that tales will warn and instruct. But you don't notice that the instruction comes, more often than not, through recognition *after* the event, rather than before it.

Besides, wolves – I don't know about people – always consider that fables really refer to others, not to themselves.'

It was this awful thought which woke me up. But fortunately the Wolf had vanished.

Literature

IBN YUSUF said:

'So many people used to come to see me with books that they had read and wanted interpreted, or books that they had written and wanted opinions about, or books of other sorts, that I was at my wits' end.

'I went to see a doctor who was also a sage. I said: "Give me some remedy for this problem."

'He gave me yet another book. This one was to show to the book-readers. Inside it contained only one phrase, and this is it: TIME WASTED READING THIS SENTENCE COULD BE EMPLOYED MORE PROFITABLY IN ALMOST ANY OTHER MANNER.'

Legend of the Nightingale

THEY tell of a man who lived in a country where there were no birds.

He travelled to another land, and there he saw and spent time in company with a nightingale. The bird taught him music.

'I shall go home and tell everyone about this marvel, and how their lives may be enriched,' he said.

'Anyone who has learned our secret', said the nightingale, 'will have to suffer the incredulity of almost everyone else. He may even have to endure something worse.'

But the man took no notice. He returned home and said to his fellows:

'I can make music.'

But those people had never heard music, and so it sounded harsh and unpleasing to their ears.

'Stop it!' they cried, 'for this deeply offends our aesthetic sense.' They asked him where he had acquired such a loathsome art, so out of keeping with what they knew to be propriety and enjoyment.

'In a far country; and, what is more, I had it from a nightingale, a singing bird.'

They quickly hanged him, because even if there were nightingales (and everyone knew that all birds were imaginary beings) this music was obviously a nasty thing.

But this is, fortunately, a story not about us, but rather from those stupid people of The Land of Fools.

Inner Senses

A CERTAIN Sufi was asked:

'Why is it that people have no inner senses?'

He said:

'O man of high promise! If they had *no* inner senses, they would not even appear to be people at all. When people lack inner sense, they behave in a completely destructive or totally passive manner. Being *aware* of an inner sense is another matter.'

Grain

THE chicken had his wish, and was magically transformed into a fox.

Then he found that he could not digest grain.

Mistakes

A CERTAIN Sufi was asked:

'Why does that dervish over there make so many mistakes?'
He answered:

'If he made no mistakes, he would be either worshipped or ignored. He makes mistakes so that people shall ask, "Why does he do what he does?"'

'But what is the advantage of that,' asked the questioner, 'especially since he does not explain himself?'

'The advantage is that people may see that which is behind him, and not the man himself as they imagine him to be.'

Mixed Behaviour

I WAS present when a visitor begged leave to ask a question, and Rais-i-Kabir gave permission for this.

The visitor said:

'What I have heard of you gives me no confidence in you. By behaving in an exaggerated manner you make people uneasy about you. Even your friends confess that they do not know how to defend you. Whatever your successes, your name will not be remembered if your conduct is as mixed as it is.'

The Rais said:

'Dear friend, one purpose of mixed behaviour is for people to notice how easily they are affected by it. A person who is affected by my smile or frown is like a polo-ball, struck in any direction by a blow, irrespective of his own character.

'Exaggerated behaviour which makes people uneasy says nothing about the behaver – but it says everything about the uneasy person. Friends seeking to defend one are serving one's interests when defence is necessary to the defended person. When the act of defending is necessary to the defending friend, then the friend is acting for his own self, not for the person whom he is defending.'

The visitor said:

'This has been a lifting of veils for me, and I am grateful, and I beg your forgiveness. But how many people will know these truths, and how few will learn them?'

Rais-i-Kabir said:

'If only one person knows it, the knowledge is still represented among men. And if it is preserved so that it shall be universal in a time beyond ours, is this not itself a thing of great goodness?'

He recited this passage:

A man wading in flooded land with a sack of corn was told,
'Drop that useless burden and save yourself!' He answered:
'If I lose that which is useless now and will be essential in
future, saving myself will be without value!'

Difficulty

ONE of the Sufi ancients declared:

'Three kinds of people are the most difficult to teach: those who are delighted that they have achieved something; those who, after learning something, are depressed that they did not know it earlier; those who are so anxious to feel progress that they cease to be sensitive to progress.'

The Greatest Vanity

ABU HALIM FARFAR said:

'The greatest vanity is to believe that one is sincere in seeking knowledge when in reality one is seeking only personal pleasure.'

'But how', asked one of those present, can a person know whether he is a victim of this malady?'

Farfar said:

'He is *not* a victim of this malady if he is content with the attention which the Master gives him; and if he is not agitated if he receives none; and if he is not disturbed at the sight of others receiving attention from the Master, and if he values even a word or a sign from the Master at its true worth – as if he were the *only* recipient of a valuable hidden treasure.'

Secret Teaching

ONE of the Sufi masters was asked:

'While your beliefs and school are known, your teachings are secret, given only to those whom you desire, and nobody is allowed to be present as an observer at your meetings, unlike the practices of the philosophers, who allow, indeed welcome, hearers of all kinds. What is the explanation of this?'

He said:

'Light of my eyes! Teaching is like charity: it is to be given secretly for the reason that the public display of charity is bad for the giver, for the receiver and for the observer. Teaching is like a nutrition, and its effects are not visible at the time it is being given, so there is no point in there being an observer except of the fruit of the nutrition. Teaching, again, is not to be considered as separated from the circumstances in which it is given. Therefore, if there are observers, their presence changes the circumstances and also therefore the effect of the teaching. If the effect of the presence of an audience were to increase the beneficial effect of teaching, then I and everyone else would have welcomed and demanded such an audience. And, fourthly, teaching varies with the Sufi dictum of the necessity for "right time, right place, right people". To ask even for information about knowledge is like throwing a lifeless carcass into fresh water: the intention may be good, but the result will be poisonous.'

The inquirer said:

'I understand what you say, but I wish to remark that this is not the manner in which ordinary teaching is carried out.'

The teacher replied:

'God grant that ordinary teaching may indeed one day be carried out in this manner! When that comes to pass we shall have no need to see any division between Sufi and other teaching!'

Working Together

SOMEONE asked Ajmal ibn Arif:

'Can you give me an example of "things apparently opposed which are really working together"?'

Ajmal said:

'The person who denounces real Sufis is apparently opposed to them. But he may, unwittingly, be working with them; for he is attracting undesirables to himself and cannot really prevent valuable people from listening to the real Sufis.'

'But', continued the questioner, 'is he not sowing doubts in the hearts of good people, and prejudicing them against the real Sufis?'

'Doubt', said Ajmal, 'is sown on doubt already existing. The hearts of good people are not places where the seed of opposition to real Sufis can possibly be sown.'

A House to which the Key is Lost

THEY asked a great Sufi:

'What is the likeness of pursuing the practices given by the ancients, in our present situation?'

The Sufi said:

'It is as the similitude of being in a house to which the key is lost. A locksmith may have to be called. Or it is as the likeness of eating the root, when the fruit and the seed have perished.

'And it is the likeness of looking at a farm, and imagining from ignorance that the road leading to it, and the rubbish dump, and the well – all necessary things – are the operation itself, as if they themselves were a growing and a being.'

Hali in Converse with an Inquirer

'Is a man worse than a scorpion?'

'Infinitely. Everyone knows that a scorpion has a sting. But the sting of a man may consist in seemingly fair words. You must know a man well before you know whether his words are stings. How well do you need to know a scorpion?'

The Observances

A MAN named Khalil said:

'I waited for years to be allowed to take part in the ceremonies, the sacred dance, even the musical recitals of the dervishes. But Arif Anwar, the Murshid (Guide) never admitted me. I am known as a wise man. But I have never really been in the School.'

Afifi, who was successor to the Murshid Anwar, said to him:

'It was from compassion for man, and through love for you, that the Arif protected you from these things.'

Khalil asked:

'How can it be "protection" to be denied the company of the elect? How can it be "love" to be excluded from those things which only enemies of the Path decry?'

Afifi answered:

'You mistake the caperings of the exhibitionist, the self-indulgence of the aesthete, and the self-deception of the imagined disciple and imagining master for the Road to Truth of the teaching. No teacher will exclude anyone from anything for which he is fitted; though he may postpone his participation, as with donkeys fenced off from carrots. For unready people, the company of the Elect becomes a burden which they cannot bear. Like a thirsty man, the more they desire it the less they can stomach it.

'It is a celestial kindness which allows "sincere imitators" to abound. They form groups and are made content by imitation. The unregenerate man attending True Practices, in the presence of a True Teacher, will be split asunder. Anwar preserved you, in your rawness, from exposure to this strain.'

The Cupboard

ONE of the followers of Musa Arkani said:

'Why must we endure such pinpricks as the actions of this idiot who has taken it upon himself to attack us so often, claiming that we are foolish, self-deluded and at the same time trying to exploit others?'

Arkani said:

'The behaviour of the environment is a manifestation of the environment. We have opened a cupboard full of delicacies. A dog has darted forward and is yapping and snapping. But we all know why dogs do these things. They do them because of their nature: the occasion is unimportant to them.

'But suppose it had been a giant bear? You would by now have been crushed to death – and therefore in no condition to indulge in the luxury of being annoyed by curs.'

What has to Be

A CERTAIN Sufi was reproached by a visitor for his stern behaviour.

He said:

'Dear friend! It took me twenty years of study and practice to learn firmness and stern behaviour, both of them very much against my nature. Now you, because you have had no such experience, expect me to become like you again.'

Generous and Humble

THIS interchange took place between Hariri and a visitor:

'Is it better to be generous or to be humble?'

'Which would you rather be?'

'I envy both kinds of people.'

'Envy of a good characteristic is worse than envy of a bad one. This is because envy is envy. When envy is directed towards good, it is an attack upon good. When envy is directed towards evil, it is in its proper place, and may be seen for what it is.'

'Then what should I do?'

'You should make sure that you are sincere. In that way you will become both humble and generous. Sincerity has no place for envy.'

Books and Sages

A MAN started visiting a Sufi. After they had had two meetings, the visitor said:

'Last time I was here you were immersed in the affairs of the congregation. This time, I am glad to see, you are dealing with something more permanent – the organization of the Order's estates.'

The Sufi said:

'Your interest in our shifting concerns is delightful to contemplate.'

The Visitor went away, feeling happy that he had pleased the Sufi.

One of the disciples asked:

'In what way was his concern for organizational matters pleasing?'

The Sufi said:

'It reminded me of the delight which I felt when my children were young. The first day their teacher started to speak of mathematics, they did not like the lesson because he dealt with "one orange plus one orange equals two oranges" – and they wanted something more serious than "mere oranges".

'Later, they were pleased because in the very next lesson he happened to say: "Two books, plus two books – equals four books." They said: "Now we are getting to the real thing – he is talking about books!"

'The dunderhead we have just seen, whose grandfather, as it were, never suspected that the Sufi Way may be taught by any activity – or sometimes perhaps none – is a suitable candidate for charity. It is a charity to please by appearing pleased.'

Two Scholars and a Sufi

Two scholars were talking. The first Scholar said:

'I have written two hundred books, and people are respectful towards me as a great scholar. But you, who have written only one small book – people regard you as a wonder.'

The second Scholar said: 'My book is a jewel, and people give it corresponding appreciation.'

'Alas!' said a Sufi, who was sitting in the corner of the room, until then unobserved, 'vanity has prevented each of you from realizing the true situation.'

The men of letters turned upon him in fury. At first they vented their spleen upon the dervish, but he did not reply. When they had unburdened themselves of their anger, curiosity began to take hold of them, and they said:

'Tell us, then, how we are to be judged, if it is not by the excellence of our works.'

'Let us think not of books, but of beautiful robes,' said the Sufi, 'and I will tell you a story.'

'There was once a man who made robes for almost all the kings of the earth, and everyone had heard of him. Then, one day, another man made a single robe – of no great magnificence, but excellent enough. This single robe was adopted by a certain dandy, and it became well known as a consequence. The people who had known the maker of this garment before he started his career were correspondingly impressed, and they honoured him, and regarded him as a wonder, a man chosen from among them for special distinction, upon whom fortune had smiled.

'And, one day, when the first robemaker appeared in the midst of these people, crying "If you honour *him*, how much more you must think of *me* – for *I* clothe all the kings of Islam!" – when this happened, nobody turned aside from their salutations to the maker of the solitary garment. The reason was, dear friends, that the maker of robes for all the kings on earth is too far away, too lofty, beyond the perception of the humble man. But to make just one robe, to have it selected by one man, to be rewarded for it: these are things which everyone can understand.'

Command

A CERTAIN Sufi was asked by a man who was attending him:

'You insist upon discipline and obedience and service of the Master. You demand that we do exactly what you command, and that we never vary a command, or criticize or oppose any individual.'

The Sufi said:

'That is a true description of what I have required.'

'But', said the other man, 'there seems to be no value in this, since you never command, and you do not give orders, and therefore we have no way of obeying you.'

The Sufi said:

'All this training is for your own sake, and for the sake of the work, this affair of ours. If it were for my sake, I would command and make you obey me. But because it is for *you*, and the command is for the sake of the Command, I have to make certain that you will obey, and that you *can* serve and that you can withhold criticism.

'These qualities are required for the time when they are required, and the occasion when they are required, not as something which is tested continually. If you have them, you have them. If you have not, acquire them by action and study. Obedience, for example, is not learnt only by obeying me. It may be by obeying the circumstances in which you are set.

'It will go hard for you when these qualities are needed, if you do not have them then. Having them is what is important. Merely displaying them is another matter.'

Incurring Blame

'Why,' asked a disciple of a Sufi, 'why does the dervish incur blame?'

'He may incur blame', said his teacher, 'to expose to the general audience how ready people are to blame others, so that the observers may see this in themselves and be less likely to adopt this fault. He may attract reproach in order to reveal the baseness of certain blamers who otherwise conceal their true characteristics. But, just as a snake may look beautiful when basking, and needs fear or an attractive prey before he shows his inner nature, so the envious and the disappointed needs a defenceless-seeming man, or other attractive morsel, before he will abandon his mild outer countenance.'

Success

A MAN went to a Sufi and said:

'Teach me how to be successful.'

The Sufi said:

'I will teach you more than that. I shall teach you to be generous to the unsuccessful. That will pave the way towards your own success, and give you far more. I shall also teach you how to be generous towards the successful; otherwise you will be liable to become bitter and unable to work towards success.'

Three Possible Reasons

A DERVISH was sitting by the roadside when a haughty courtier with his retinue, riding past in the opposite direction, struck him with a cane, shouting:

'Out of the way, you miserable wretch!'

When they had swept past, the dervish rose and called after them:

'May you attain all that you desire in the world, even up to its highest ranks!'

A bystander, much impressed by this scene, approached the devout man and said to him:

'Please tell me whether your words were motivated by generosity of spirit, or because the desires of the world will undoubtedly corrupt that man even more?'

'O man of bright countenance,' said the dervish, 'has it not occurred to you that I said what I did because people who attain their real desires would not need to ride about striking dervishes?'

Healing

A DERVISH was once asked:

'How can you heal the sick, when your own Master cannot?' He said:

'A man was once asked, "Why do you walk to the grocer's shop, when your Master does not do so?" And the man replied, "It is because my Master is making bread that I am walking to the shop. If he were not engaged in baking, there would be no need of flour."'

Dialogue

A DISCIPLE asked the deputy of a dervish:

'Why has so-and-so not been through the Phase of Acquiring Patience?'

He said:

'The test of his patience is you – for you ask questions all the time, while he has no need of other tests in that direction in this place of study.'

The disciple then asked:

'But when do *I* begin my exercises in developing humility, which is said to be my need?'

The deputy told him:

'Just as you are a source of exercise in patience to him, he is a source of developing humility for you. Enduring you should help to make him patient. Observing your own attitude towards him should help to make *you* humble. It is not humility to demand to be made humble.'

Meatballs

AWAD AFIFI was asked:

'Which kinds of worldly happening can conduce towards the understanding of the Sufi Way?'

He said:

'I shall give you an illustration when it is possible.'

Some time later, Awad and some of his group were on a visit to a garden outside their city.

A number of rough mountaineer nomads were encamped by the wayside. Awad stopped and bought a small piece of roast meat from one nomad, who had set up a Kebab stall there.

As he raised the meat to his lips, the stall-keeper uttered a cry and fell to the ground in a strange state. Then he stood up, took Awad's hand and kissed it.

Awad said:

'Let us be on our way.' Accompanied by the roast-meat man, all proceeded along the highroad.

This nomad's name was Koftapaz (meatball-cook) and he was soon revealed as one whose *baraka*, spiritual power, gave meaning and effect to the spiritual exercises of the whole School.

Awad called his followers together and said:

'I have been asked which kind of worldly happening can conduce towards the understanding of the Sufi Way.

'Let those who were present at the meeting with Koftapaz tell those who were not there, and then let Koftapaz himself give the explanation, for he is now my appointed Deputy.'

When all had been informed about the encounter on the way to the garden, Sheikh Koftapaz stood up and said:

'O people upon whom the shadow of the beneficent bird

Simurgh has rested! Know that all my life I have been a maker of meatballs.

'Therefore it was easy for me to know the Master by the way in which he raised a morsel to his lips – for I had seen the inwardness of every other kind of mortal by his outwardness; and if you are totally accomplished in your own work, you may recognize your Imam (leader) by his relationship with your work.'

At the Crossroads

A SUFI was sitting at a crossroads one morning when a young man came up to him and asked whether he could study with him.

'Yes, for one day,' said the Sufi.

Throughout the day, one traveller after another stopped to ask questions about man and life, about Sufism and Sufis, or to beg for help – or just to pay respects.

But the Sufi wanderer merely sat in an attitude of contemplation, his head on his knee, and he made no answer at all. One by one, the people went away.

Towards evening a poor man with a heavy bundle approached the pair and asked the way to the nearest town. The Sufi immediately stood up, took the man's burden on his own shoulders and conducted him a part of the way along the right road. Then he returned to the crossroads.

The young disciple asked:

'Was that man, miserable peasant though he looked, really a saint in disguise, one of the secret wanderers of high rank?'

The Sufi sighed and said:

'He was the only person whom we have seen today who really sought the object which he claimed to want.'

Poems

A WANDERER said to a Sufi poet:

'Your verses are recited everywhere, but your growing fame annoys as many people as it pleases. Can there be a purpose in this?'

He said:

'Beloved of the Brethren! There may or may not be a purpose, but how instructive is an examination of the *effect*!

'The Sufi is like the tree which gives shade for relief and wood for use and fruit for pleasure and nutrition.

'Now, if a man is annoyed by a tree, observers may be able to realize how stupid he is, and consequently be able to avoid him. The hostile critic thinks that the tree is a snake standing up to strike – for his enmity distorts his vision.

'People of sense will withdraw from the company of such an unfortunate one. And there will be at least some who say:

"Is that not a tree rather than a snake?"

'Such people will draw near to a tree which, even with their sensibility, they might have overlooked before.

'Have you not heard of the man who said: "If this horrid man says that Zaid is to be opposed, I will draw closer to Zaid, for he must assuredly have qualities which I have not suspected."?'

Discernment

A VISITOR who was also a famous philosopher said to Bahaudin Naqshband:

'I have read widely and fully of the spiritual practices which can transform ordinary men into Perfect Ones.'

Bahaudin said:

'You would have done better to read of the stages and the states in which the Perfect Men can come into being. But your desire for perfection may be like the ambition of the farmer who knew that flour came from wheat but was too attached to the thought of flour to till the soil, and so he starved.'

The visitor said:

'Did the farmer have nobody to reproach him with the shallowness of his thinking?'

Bahaudin answered:

'Indeed he did. A wise man came to him and said: "You are not going deep enough into this matter." And the farmer replied: "You could have accused me of shallowness if I had wanted bread and only gone so far back as the flour. But see! I have gone beyond flour, even as far as wheat!" That was the nature of their conversation.'

The visitor said:

'In the house of one of your disciples I have met people whom you have sent out, and who are of the nature of saints, and their sanctity is resplendent, and I find none like this in your own house, here.'

Bahaudin sighed and said:

'In the house of the jeweller there are unpolished gems; and those who delight in the colour of gold in the shop may be incapable of discerning it in the mine.'

Camels and Bridges

ONE of the first people to be called Sufi was a man whom few people understood. One day a visitor went to this Sufi's chief disciple and said:

'Why does the Sufi send away so many people? Most spiritual men regard it as an obligation to teach all who come. Why does he not endure the burden, so that he might help others?'

It is related that the chief disciple took the inquirer to a bridge where heavily-laden camels were crossing. He said:

'Now look and ask yourself the question again. Seeing this bridge and those camels, ask in the language of camels and bridges:

' "Why do the camels not carry a heavier burden? Why does the bridge not endure more?" '

Interchange

A DERVISH was approached by a total stranger who handed him a piece of cloth.

Without hesitation, the dervish reached into a basket and gave the man a fish out of it.

The many young men who surrounded the dervish to absorb his wisdom held heated discussions as to the symbolic or other meaning of these actions.

Then, after many days, the dervish had them tell him what their several conclusions had been. Then he said:

'The real substance of the interchange was to enable me to choose those of you who are sufficiently masters of understanding to see that this was a meaningless interchange!'

Mosquitoes

A DERVISH said to a Sufi:

'You make yourself difficult to find. But this does not only select the best people, the people of feeling, to seek you: it encourages the idle, those who try to find you just because it *is* difficult.'

'Why should there be any harm in that?' asked the Sufi. 'The people of true perception have in any case arrived at the door, and that is correct. The ridiculous ones must always have an object, and will seek anything difficult – whether it is me or not. But it is easy to send the ridiculous on their way, since their finding a Sufi physically may be possible for them, while finding him spiritually is impossible for them.

'We can fight wolves and admit to our company rational men: but a superabundance of witless mosquitoes could choke us. And nobody would benefit from that.'

How to Become a Thief

ONCE upon a time there was a man who was a religious bigot; he was small and had a rather crabbed face and believed that everything which he was must be the result of divine influence alone.

One day when he was sitting thinking to himself how good he was, a tall and burly thief came up to him. The thief said: 'I am a thief.'

At first the man was annoyed, then amazed, then reproachful, but the thief was there to play on the man's vanity. He started to say such things as, 'You are too small to be a thief – but I could make you the fastest runner in the world.'

In short, the bigot became interested in the thief's promises, and his greed attached itself to a new ambition, to become a runner and jumper.

Every day the thief visited the bigot, and every day there was more running and higher jumping. Finally, such were the praises lavished upon him, the bigot decided to accompany the thief on a burglary.

They climbed the wall of the Sultan's palace, they outstripped the pursuing guard, climbed a tower and leapt onto the roof of the audience-chamber where a giant ruby hung suspended above the throne, in total darkness. Just as they were reaching for the ruby, they were seized by guards, lamps were brought and the hall was seen to be full of people.

The king asked the thief what he was doing. 'Your Majesty,' said the thief, 'I was caught, if you remember, some months ago. And I was released because I said that to be a thief was a matter of how people had played upon me in earlier days, and that even an upright cleric could be a thief. Your Majesty released me on condition that I made a thief out of an honest man, and brought him here. I asked the Chamberlain to have this place in darkness for the purpose of this very demonstration.'

'This is indeed a wonder,' said the king, 'when a thief has been honest enough to keep his word, and a religious man has been dishonest enough to become a thief.'

A Thousandth Part

A PIOUS but habit-ridden man one day visited one of the greatest Sufis of all time, anxious to see him before he died, greedy to obtain something from him for himself, unable to restrain his curiosity as to what his appearance might be, not capable of approaching him with calm and ease, ready to apprehend.

He said to the Sufi:

'Your Sufism intoxicates me! What I have read of your work amazes me! I had no idea that there was so much learning which had not yet been given out to mankind!'

The Sufi said:

'If what you have experienced of Sufism has cast you into such a state as this, it is just as well that you have only seen one-thousandth part of it.'

The pious man said:

'How can this be?'

'Well,' said the Sufi, 'Sufism is one-thousandth of the total of knowledge. The rest may be known to the Sufi, but it is only the thousandth particle which is seen or felt by such as you.'

The pious man said:

'What words, what thoughts, what actions! I am again lost in wonder at the grandeur of such a concept!'

The Sufi said:

'All wisdom which is employed by spectators merely for the purpose of admiration is lost upon them! Beware of admiring the peach too much, in case you find you cannot taste it. That is what is meant by "Learn how to learn".'

The Aim of the Nightingale

A NIGHTINGALE who happened to have no home of his own decided that he would try to settle in a certain forest. The birds who were already there, however, had their own ideas about the matter, and soon drove him out.

One day, sitting disconsolately by the dusty road nearby, he was spied by another nightingale, who stopped to ask why he looked so forlorn.

'I tried', said the first bird, 'to make my home among other birds, but they pecked, and they mobbed me, and they flapped at me until I had to leave yonder forest.'

'Perhaps you were boastful,' said the other nightingale. 'When, in a similar situation, I sought a tree of my own, all the birds first collected and asked me what I was doing, why I was singing.'

'Yes, those birds did the same with me,' said the first nightingale.

'And what did you say?'

'I said: "I am singing because I simply cannot help it." '

'And then?'

'And then they attacked me, as I have described.'

'Ah,' said the other bird, 'that was your mistake. They thought that you had no self-control, that you might be mad and that you might try to make them behave in a similar manner. When *I* was asked the same question, I said: "I am trying to please you with my song." *That* was an aim which they could understand.'

Abstention

A DEVOUT pilgrim travelled for many days to visit Baba Charkhi. When he arrived at his house, the pilgrim was most distressed to see that, although it was the fasting month, Charkhi was sitting in the middle of the day eating large quantities of roast meat.

Bitterly disappointed, the pilgrim nevertheless made his salutations and sat for three days with the Baba, hoping that some explanation might be offered. But there was none, and the pilgrim disconsolately started on his way home.

He had not gone far when he saw the cell of a religious man beside the road, and he stopped to say prayers and pass some time with the anchorite.

The religious man, after they had sat together for a space, said:

'You are sad, and your distress is infecting the air, so that I am unable to maintain my peace. Can it be that you have been to see Charkhi?'

The pilgrim said:

'Your perception of my state is undeniably an evidence of the holiness of your vigils! You have transformed my sorrow, by that remark, into delight, and in place of sadness I now have hope. But can you tell me what has happened to the great Charkhi, that he should behave in such a manner?'

The holy man said:

'Nothing has happened to Charkhi. I occupy myself with prayers and fastings. I sing devotional songs and carry out special practices. I am abstemious and I follow the rules which have been laid down for those who would attain. This is what you, too, should be doing, and this is what Charkhi recognized in you, this is what he said to you, by his actions.

'If I were as great a man as Charkhi, I would have no need of such things. If you were fit to become his disciple, you would not have been influenced by the appearance and insensitive to the reality. You and I are in the same dire situation. One day one or other of us, or both, may reach the stage when we can become the disciples of Baba Charkhi.'

An Obscure Scholar

AN OBSCURE scholar approached a Sufi master and asked him a stupid question.

'Be off with you!' said the Sufi.

The scholar went away, loudly maintaining that the Sufi could not be civil if he tried, and was an ignorant braggart to boot.

Another philosopher, interested by the Sufi's attitude but unsure of how to interpret it, asked the reason for his behaviour.

'Ah, friend!' said the Sufi, 'you will never interpret such conduct by the standards of "rules" which you seek to apply. You will be able to understand only by the standards of "moments".

'At that moment I had a chance to do less damage to the wiseacre by shaking him off "impatiently" than I would have done (because of his character) by refutation, reasoned arguments or any other customary alternative.'

'But what of your own repute? For instance, as a man of courtesy and restraint?'

'The repute of the gardener comes with the appearance of flowers, not with the breaking of the ground; and the repute of the farmer from the crop, and not from the threshing of seed. If they stopped their work to consider repute at every moment, would there be flowers, would there be crops?' the Sufi asked.

'Therefore the wise have said: "The silken dress gains admiration and is followed by no real product; wear, therefore, wool – until this becomes the badge of pride with evil product".'

Confined Thinking

IN a resthouse on one of the great Central Asian highways of the Silk Route, a certain man was talking, loudly and incessantly, one evening.

Everyone hoped that he would stop, so that travellers could get some rest before the following morning's early start.

But this man showed no sign of quietening down, and few of those present were pleased when a wandering dervish approached the garrulous one, greeted him politely and said:

'I wish to listen to every single word of yours with the greatest possible attention. Please continue to talk.'

The talker continued with greater volume and verbosity, phrasing his harangue with more and more virtuosity, while the dervish sat before him, his gaze fixed upon him with intense concentration.

Within a few minutes the man had almost stopped talking – and the dervish was asleep.

In the morning, as the caravan's animals were being saddled up for the march, some of the travellers asked the dervish the meaning of his behaviour. He said:

'That man wanted your attention, and you did not want to give it, because you wanted to be doing something else. *I* wanted rest, but I knew that I would have to pay for it in advance. As soon as our friend had gained his objective, he no longer wanted it. As soon as I gained mine, of relative quiet following concentrated effort, I took advantage of it – and you people benefited too.'

When asked his own impressions of the night before, the talker said:

'That pretended dervish had the insolence to fall asleep as I spoke, after pretending to be interested. He was only trying to impress us all. Let that be a lesson to you.'

The Outward and the Inward

A Sufi of Bokhara attracted large concourses of people, and his house was always full of disciples and pilgrims.

Distressed by this activity and movement, one devout student left the city almost as soon as he had entered it in search of the sage, and made his way to the hut of a more solitary contemplative in Eastern Turkestan.

When the two had sat in silent contemplation for a time, the mystic raised his head, having read his visitor's mind, and said:

'When you judge by externals, by appearances only, you will gain only superficialities.

'You disliked the outward aspect of the Sage of Bokhara, and therefore could not reach his inner aspect.

'On the Final Day, if you are to be judged in similar fashion – on your outward form, why not prepare your own outwardness? You are soberly dressed; bedeck yourself with beads. Your robe is plain – make it an object of remark. Decorate and display yourself. Then you might at least be credited with being consistent.'